Praise for *Surviving Remnant*

"There were portions that brought tears to my eyes of the trials and tribulations of the refugees…I loved the accents of the characters. I found the overall message was to demonstrate how a group of Jewish refugees…not only survived but raised their children to be successful U.S. citizens."
—David A. Field, Chairman, the Olga Lengyel Institute, Memorial Library

"I really don't know of another book that describes so well a group of *grine* — their first steps in the United States, their travails and their successes. What a great accomplishment… written so well that one is curious to know as much as possible about each of the families in the group."
—Michlean Amir, Association of Jewish Libraries

"A remarkable story, written in simple, readable style that evokes a child's voice of family love and kinship. An altogether entertaining and memorable narrative."
—Brian Jud, Executive Director, Association of Publishers for Special Sales, author of *How to Make Real Money Selling Books*

D1468643

"Through Marcus' loving recounting, the reader comes away with tremendous respect for these people who had the courage to move to a new country, learn the language and customs, remain fiercely committed to their children and become successful in their own way…I felt a warm feeling for them, as if I had made some new friends too."

—Nancy Simonds, Nancy Simonds Communication, LLC

"Hanna Marcus deftly takes us into the world of Jews trying to recuperate from the nightmare of the Holocaust as they adjust to a new life in the United States."

—Doreen Rappaport, author of *Beyond Courage: The Untold Story of Jewish Resistance During the Holocaust*

"There is so much here that still resonates today, especially Hanna's keen observations on how the use of language shapes our perceptions. Instead of 'genocide' and 'mass murder,' we have 'selection' and 'liquidation.' *Surviving Remnant* should be required reading in history and sociology classes."

—Elisabeth Petry, author of *At Home Inside: A Daughter's Tribute to Ann Petry*

"Hanna provides a warm and compelling portrait of her mother and her neighbors, showing the duality of life for the survivors, their mourning of their losses, their continuing faith, and their will to move on. A satisfying read!"

—Linda Grodofsky, Branch Supervisor, Springfield City Library

"Although the stories are unique to those immigrants during that time in our history, their aspirations are universal and inspiring."

—Diane DeFronzo, LCSW, Guardian Ad Litem

"Readers familiar with Springfield, Massachusetts will appreciate the skill Marcus brings to her recreation of this industrial city, itself in the throes of post-war change. The beauty of *Surviving Remnant*, however, lies in the universality of its story, the making of a new life...against difficult odds. The "Jewish Greenhorns" who populate this sequel are vividly and warmly portrayed."

—David Garnes, author of *After the War Was Over: A Novel of World War II*

"With clarity and compassion, the author delves into the complex lives of survivors. . . . Set in mid-20th century New England, this extremely well-written story has value to anyone who grew up as the child of a parent or among a community of people that had survived the trauma of war and were coping with a new society and country."

—Douglas McDonough, Library Director, Manchester, CT Public Library

"In this book, readers are beside the author as she tries to make sense of the world. . . . Through the lives of the adults in her community, Hanna tries to make meaning out of the remnants she finds around her. By doing so, she helps us understand the struggle of any survivor of trauma, but also shows readers the great importance of community."

—Cara Crandall, Holocaust educator and English teacher

"Challenge yourself to put on the author's shoes and step into her world of new immigrants with her grace and determination."

—Ellen Frankel, Special Education teacher, Hartford Public Schools

"I found the book…a very enjoyable read…contained many humorous touches and much pathos…many universal issues facing immigrants everywhere, especially in today's world."

—Rima Riedel, Creative Expression therapist

"We're all familiar with Anne Frank but most of us… do not know what happened to Jews who survived the Holocaust…and became immigrant refugees. *Surviving Remnant* tells one of these stories in a sometimes humorous, uplifting manner, but more importantly, from the human perspective."

☆☆☆☆☆ Five Star Review on Goodreads

Surviving Remnant

To Sue —
I hope this
story inspires
you,

Always,

Howard P. May

Surviving Remnant

Memories of the Jewish Greenhorns in 1950s America

Hanna Perlstein Marcus

Published by Buttonhole Publishing

Designed by Acorn Studio, Inc.

Most of the characters in this memoir have fictitious names but are generally based on real people or are embellished, imagined, or are composites of several individuals. In some cases, I have used the characters' real names, with their permission.

The events described in these pages are largely founded on real happenings. Some events, however, have been partially fictionalized to fit the perspective of the child at the center of the story. In those instances the depictions do not refer to real situations. As I portray them, the remembrances stem solely from my own memory as a child living among and interacting with this singular community and include neither interviews with nor the perspective of any other person.

In Chapter 1, "The Outsiders," the reference to the song "Di Grine Kusine" is to the original song with lyrics by Abe Schwartz and Khayim Prizant (published 1921); translation retrieved from the Zemerl Archives, http://www.zemerl.com.

In Chapter 3, "The Tattooed Ones," I have taken Winston Churchill's words from Sir Martin Gilbert, "Churchill and the Holocaust," *British Broadcasting Corporation (BBC),* updated on February 17, 2011, retrieved from http://www.bbc.co.uk/history/worldwars/genocide/churchill_holocaust_01.shtml.

In Chapter 5, "Surviving Remnant," Dezso Perlstein's Buchenwald Prisoner Identification Card, prisoner number 57569, from *Häftlings-Personal-Karte,* is from the International Tracing Service collection, United States Holocaust Memorial Museum, document number 6799800. The accompanying card used for men interned at the Buchenwald concentration camp lists the six documents at the camp under his prisoner number. ITS collection, USHMM, document number 6799799.

The final quotation in Chapter 10, "The Shul," is from Adele Berlin, Mark Zvi Brettler, and Michael Fishbane (editors), *The Jewish Study Bible: Jewish Publication Society Tanakh Translation,* New York: Oxford University Press, 2004, p. 900.

The revelation about the Barts in Chapter 33, "The Freedom Fighters," is from Michael Bart and Laurel Corona, *Until Our Last Breath: A Holocaust Story of Love and Partisan Resistance,* New York: St. Martin's Press, 2008.

Unless otherwise credited, all the illustrations that appear in the book are the author's.

ISBN-13: 978-0-9979712-0-0
ISBN-10: 0-9979712-0-7

To my grandparents, Hani and Simon Perlstein of Dámóc,
Hungary, for raising an exceptional family and
giving me my mother, Sidonia, and . . .

To the greenhorns, for providing me with a model of
courage, resilience, and sheer determination —
and the need to tell their American story.

They count as quite forgot;

They are as men who have existed not;

Theirs is a loss past loss of fitful breath;

It is the second death . . .

But what has been will be —

First memory, then oblivion's swallowing sea;

Like men forgone, shall we merge into those

Whose story no one knows.

Thomas Hardy, "The To-Be-Forgotten," parts 4 and 6

Contents

Prologue: The Show. xi

Part One: Initiation

  1 – The Outsiders 17

  2 – The Arrival. 23

  3 – The Tattooed Ones. 31

  4 – The Matchmaker 37

  5 – Surviving Remnant 43

  6 – The Broken Angel. 49

  7 – The Unfortunate Affair .53

  8 – The Citizens. 59

  9 – The Club. 65

 10 – The Shul 69

 11 – Faithful Friends. 79

 12 – The Lucky One 85

 13 – Yuri's Story. 89

 14 – The Power of Education 91

 15 – Restitution of a Life 99

 16 – A Community Still Vulnerable 111

Part Two: Acculturation

 17 – The Girl of Summer. 119

 18 – Clair de Lune. 127

 19 – The Matchmaker: Progress Report 1 131

 20 – The Somnambulist. 133

 21 – Scenes From a Communal Life 137

 22 – Outings. 145

 23 – The Card Counter 149

 24 – The Matchmaker: Progress Report 2 153

 25 – Patterns and Styles 157

 26 – Nerves. 163

 27 – The Brownie 169

 28 – The Matchmaker: Progress Report 3 173

Part Three: Revelations

29 – The Somber Romantic...................... 177
30 – The Matchmaker: Progress Report 4 183
31 – The Games............................... 187
32 – The Coin Collector........................ 191
33 – The Freedom Fighters 195
34 – The Ring................................ 201
35 – The Farm 205
36 – Reinvention............................. 209
37 – The Matchmaker: A Revelation and a Warning,
         Progress Report 5 215
38 – The Forever Kind of Gratitude............... 221
39 – Illegal Inventory 225

Part Four: Maturation

40 – The Facts of Life 231
41 – The Last Bachelor......................... 235
42 – The "H" Chain 241
43 – The Fever 247
44 – The Promotion 253
45 – The Big Move 257
46 – The Debut 261
47 – The Car................................. 265
48 – Restitution: The Meandering Conclusion 269

Epilogue: The Final Show........................ 283

Acknowledgments............................... 289

Prologue: The Show

*D*a *show vill start in ten minutes,* announced a woman in broken English while banging on our door. Before we could even open it, we heard her loud footsteps as she sprinted down the stairs. I was not interested in seeing the show again. *What's to see?* The boy had performed his act many times, and while it was true that it was always a big hit in our community, I did not need to see it another time.

But Hanele, my mother groaned in her still-thick Hungarian accent, *ve have to go or else everyvon gonna tink ve are stuck up!*

Okay, okay, I'll go, but this is the last time, I said, while pouting and rolling my eyes.

We went down the three flights of stairs that reeked from the mouse cemetery amid its treads. Then we walked outside to the rear section of our building, where the apartments on Osgood Street were quite a bit smaller than our two-bedroom unit. The warm, breezy mid-summer day had already turned into near dusk when most of the adults were home from work and families had already eaten their supper. It could not have been more convenient or economical to see a free show right in our own building and, at the same time, one suitable for adults to take their kids.

As we walked into the Landsmans' tiny kitchen, we observed that about twenty people, adults and children, had already crowded into the room and spilled out into the adjacent hallway. Almost every inch of space was occupied, some people seated at the kitchen table, some on folding chairs, and many just standing wherever a piece of floor was still available. After our arrival, five or six more eager attendees opened the screen door and inched into the over-flowing crowd. They must have been standing on one foot or floating on air.

The mother and father were roaming the small, packed room as best they could, chatting with each person about the wonderful show they were about to see, so proud of their only child's ability to elicit the raucous laughter they had seen at previous shows. *Just vait,* his mother said, *It's gonna be even better den last time. You tink Milton Berle is funny? Dis is just unbelievable!*

Soon, the boy came out of his bedroom, which was also the family dining room, and gave his enraptured audience a big smile. I wondered how the spectators could be so excited about a show many of them had seen several times before, but they hooted and hollered at him as though he were, in fact, Milton Berle.

He was a tiny, dark-haired boy with big brown eyes, smaller than most boys his age, which was seven, the same age as me. As he stood in front of the kitchen sink wearing a short-sleeved, multi-colored shirt that hung outside his brown pants, he looked around without saying a word, smiling at each person.

Then, with no introduction, while the audience was fervently shouting his name, he proceeded slowly to unbutton his shirt, finally ripping it off to reveal a naked chest and torso underneath. He stuck out his chest as far as it would go, revealing not much more than skin and bones. He was so skinny that when he did this, each bone was clearly delineated; the audience could see his full rib cage as though it were an x-ray image. He might have been even skinnier than he had been at his earlier performances.

Despite my initial reluctance to attend this bizarre event, the intense laughter of everyone in the room seemed to rub off on me. We all remained laughing for the next few minutes as the boy turned from side to side and front to back displaying his emaciated upper body. Some of the adult attendees were even pointing at him with awe and loudly talking to each other in Yiddish about the phenomenon they had just witnessed, as though they had never seen anything like it before in their lives. *Oy, er iz azoy moyger* [Oh, he is so skinny]!

The boy's parents were beaming from ear to ear and whispered to several of the spectators, *See, ve told you it vould be unbelievable.* The exhibit was over in a matter of minutes, but the crowd lingered for another hour or so to continue to kibitz with one another about this extraordinary spectacle and to have a glass of tea and coffee cake baked by the boy's mother, the best cook in the community.

My mother and I stayed for just a little while, long enough to eat a piece of the homemade cake, but then, at my insistence, we left to go back to our apartment. *Okay, Hanele, ve came, ve saw. Now ve can go*, my mother said, having never heard of Julius Caesar. We had met our obligation to attend the show, and my mother was satisfied we had not turned up our noses at the popular event. I have to admit, though, in spite of my resistance, we did our share of laughing along with the rest of the audience.

Nothing produced such delight among the *grine* as Yussie's body exhibition. Not even Milton Berle. The irony of it all was that only a decade earlier, the same adults in the room who had erupted in wild spontaneous amusement at the sight of the gaunt figure, had each looked just like him. So what was so funny? I was not able to figure that out for some time to come.

Part One: Initiation

CHAPTER 1

The Outsiders

None of them was related to me by blood. Yet they surrounded me like the sea around a lost fish. Having no living grandparents, aunts, uncles, siblings, or even a father, I would have been a very lonely child without them.

My mother and I were different from many of the other members of our community because we were not part of any nuclear or extended family. An air of mystery surrounded us pertaining to the identity of my father, who was noticeably absent, and our silence about the events that had led to our circumstances.

Although it has been more than fifty years since the greenhorns were my whole world, they remain in my memory as though my time with them were yesterday. Yet those fifty years had also caused my perceptions to become muddled, both vague and sharp. Today, recalling those faces, characters, and events, somehow I have been able to piece together the details of their first dozen years in America with much more insight and clarity than I ever could before. In the process, I have allowed myself to read between the lines of those actions and ways of behaving that I took only at face value as a child and portray the refugees in the insular world of my childhood as the sympathetic yet strong-minded and resilient individuals they were.

Americans called them the "greenhorns," symbolic of a calf's budding green horns, a name Americans used for any immigrant who arrived on their shores. Using the Yiddish term *di grine* to refer to themselves, the members of my community were outsiders in a strange land whose language they had yet to speak fluently. Most of the *grine* I knew had immigrated to Springfield, Massachusetts, around 1949 from myriad European displaced person camps, where for several years in the aftermath of World War II they were sheltered.

I have always felt closer to the greenhorns than to any other group of which I have ever been a part. Indeed, my attachment to many members of the *grine* brought about my decade-long quest to find a suitable husband and father for my mother and me among them.

Maybe all of us reflect on the community of our childhoods, the distinctive characters that populated the community, the various dwelling units, the neighborhood places and events that shaped our youth, and the dark secrets we swore never to reveal to anyone. Yet, I have always thought my community was like no other since all its adult members, and some of the older children, were survivors of one of the most heinous events that has ever occurred on the face of the earth. After the Holocaust, the survivors came to a new land, one they had only heard about in their native countries — countries to which they could no longer return.

The popular Jewish folk song written in 1921 about "Di Grine Kuzine," the greenhorn cousin, describes a young Jewish European woman who, like many immigrants, arrives on America's shores with dreams of a land of Paradise. Once she was as "beautiful as gold" with "cheeks red as oranges." Yet after a while in America, she becomes disillusioned with the land of her dreams. In the end, she is bitter and derisive about her new home. The song exemplifies how, despite the overwhelmingly optimistic stories about the fate of immigrants in America, their lives often did not result in comfortable surroundings and unimaginable riches.

As it happened, my grandfather had also come to America from Hungary in the late nineteenth century as an adolescent, only to turn back to his little village after nine months in New York City, equivalent to the time he had spent in his mother's womb. He carried with him his disappointment, which came from his observations of an immigrant's hard life and his perceived erosion of traditional Jewish values in the new world. In a twist of fate, his insistence on returning to Hungary placed him and his family in the eye of the storm over fifty years later.

In contrast, my *grine* were, indeed, newcomers to a land they may have once imagined in their earlier lives, yet unlike the "grine kuzine" and my grandfather, they ultimately viewed their adopted land from a kinder perspective, determined to attain success and achieve contented lives in their new country.

It was not a sad community on the surface. On the contrary, to the casual observer, they were a happy bunch, smiles always on their faces and telling funny stories. They held parties for any and every occasion. It did not have to be in honor of a monumental event or national holiday for them to get together in someone's small apartment, set up tables and chairs for food and drink, and wish someone *l'chaim* ('cheers,' or literally, 'to life') or *mazel tov* (commonly used as a wish for good fortune) for a fifth birthday or grade school academic achievement. After observing those cheerful occasions, I needed a long time to fathom the culture shock they must have experienced upon their arrival in America.

When they arrived in the late 1940s and early 1950s from the labor and death camps of the Holocaust, they were met by America's misguided reaction to the new refugees. People encouraged them to forget the loss of their families and the torture they had endured on the European continent. It would be best to move on, people advised, to build new futures for themselves and the children they had produced after the war. Americans urged them to try to erase the past and to focus solely on the present, supposedly as part of the healing process.

However, no human being could forget the kind of cruelty and insane violence they had suffered. Instead of finding ways to allow the survivors to process their innumerable losses, society preferred to bury them as though the events had never occurred. It was this mostly well-intentioned yet shortsighted view of the aftereffects of trauma that enhanced the bond between the *grine* that no one else could ever understand. Thus, their pervasive humor was, in part, a cover for their painful secrets, and partly due to their determination to live the rest of their lives in the pursuit of happiness.

The Springfield Committee for New Americans settled most of them in the north end of the city, where housing costs were lower than in other neighborhoods but living quarters were still clean and habitable. By 1950, many of these immigrant families lived in a 1920s era apartment building at 64-68 Osgood Street near the corner of Dwight Street, one of the main arteries of the city, not too far from the old Springfield Hospital.

Although their backgrounds ranged from cultured, cosmopolitan settings to rural, less educated areas, their common experiences as victims and survivors of the Holocaust brought them together. In a way, the multiple families who lived in close quarters on Osgood Street became similar to the Jewish communal environments of the *shtetls*, the small market towns of Eastern Europe, where Jews had lived for centuries before World War II. Everyone looked out for one another.

The delicious food they prepared ranged from savory *kreplach* filled with meat or potatoes to sweet *kugel* and *blintzes*, all without regard to calories or fat content. Although most of the *grine* were Polish, quite a few were from other European countries, including Germany, Hungary, Lithuania, and other central or Eastern European lands. Since they spoke many native languages, their best means of communication was Yiddish, the common mother tongue whose roots went back to the Middle Ages and was familiar to most European Jews.

I know now that the members of the *grine* were not as simple or jovial as they seemed to a child's eyes. Undercurrents, like the memories of past lives, struggles in the new world, murdered families, misguided relationships, physical infirmities, mental breakdowns, and loneliness were thick in the air. These days, I wonder how they managed to adjust to being outsiders in a foreign land. Did their sorrow lead them to make serious errors in judgment after the war and even during their first few years in America? Given their common past, did they find positive ways of relating to their children, born after World War II? And did they compensate for the losses still so fresh in their minds and easily assimilate into American society? Indeed, this immigrant group was much more nuanced and complex than I had imagined.

CHAPTER 2

The Arrival

The USAT *General R. L. Howze,* named after the famed Spanish American War and World War I hero, was formerly a naval warship during World War II, carrying American troops and Japanese prisoners to various destinations to and from the Pacific. After the war, it was converted to an army transport vessel carrying displaced persons to their new countries. The General Howze brought us from the northern port of Bremerhaven, Germany, to New York Harbor on July 3, 1949, on the eve of American Independence Day. Sometimes, when I was older, I kidded my mother about whether she thought the fireworks we observed as we approached the harbor were in honor of our arrival instead of the Fourth of July celebrations.

My mother often reminded me of the rough ten-day crossing from Germany to America, marked by the boat's pronounced, turbulent rocking, which produced ubiquitous seasickness, filling the air with a pungent, putrid odor. As a woman and young child, we were accommodated in the third cabin of the ship, where perhaps quarters were roomier, but also closer to the bow, where odors and movements were even more pronounced. Originally built to hold more than three thousand military personnel during wartime, as a transport vessel its cargo dropped to about seven hundred immigrants sailing to new harbors. Only twenty-two months old at the time of the voyage, I could not remember it, but my mother's keen storytelling skills always brought it to life.

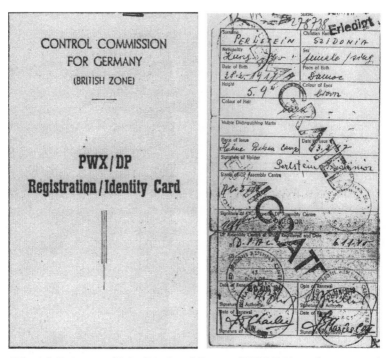

Sidonia's Prisoner of War/Displaced Person (PWX/DP) card, cover, and contents

As a child, it was easy for me to identify the things my mother had brought with her on the ship. They included only the few items she had acquired during her four-year stay at the Bergen Belsen displaced persons (DP) camp, such as her two goose-down comforters; a few pieces of Rosenthal china; enameled pots and pans; photographs of her time at the DP camp; candelabra to light the "Shabbos" candles; and most precious of all, her Köhler console sewing machine. It was this last item that would prove to be the most vital during our next fifty years in America. Noticeably absent were any items from her homeland, Hungary. They were all left behind when her family was wrenched from home.

Her brown-leather clutch purse held many of the documents she had carried with her during four years as a displaced person. One of the primary documents was her Prisoner of War/Displaced Person (PWX/DP) Registration/Identity Card, stamped multiple times by the Displaced Persons Assembly Centre Staff, and marked "EMIGRATED" in big bold letters at the time of her departure. She held her clutch bag tightly as though to safeguard her identity papers to prove at any time her and her child's status as eligible permanent residents of the United States.

Just as we had come in July of 1949, many other immigrants arrived during the same year aboard various transport ships destined for numerous cities around the world, primarily in Australia, Canada, Israel, Mexico, New Zealand, South Africa, South America, and the United States. Since President Harry Truman had signed the Displaced Persons Act of 1948 (Public Law 80-774) into law, many DP's saw the United States as finally lifting its long-held quotas and welcoming the victims of persecution into the land. We were among about a hundred of those families that had immigrated to Springfield, Massachusetts.

My mother's first letter to her wealthy Beverly Hills relatives, sent even before she left Germany, had asked for their assistance.

It fell on deaf ears. Discovering their address through an intermediary who helped survivors link to relatives in America, she had
received a response, but also a stern refusal of her request for aid.
Yet, my mother felt the need to try again to appeal to their sense of
charity and sympathy. Their second response to her pleas, written
by my mother's cousin's wife, received after our arrival in America,
produced the following strange, ethereal letter, in Hungarian:

April 17, 1950

Dear Szidi:

*In the meantime the spring has come. Since the last time we
heard from each other nothing has changed around here. I'm
struggling to survive.*

*I hope I will get good news from you soon. How did you
spend the Easter holidays? How is the child? My son turned 17
on the 14th of this month. May God help him to grow up strong
and healthy and able to be independent shortly.*

I wish you all the best together with the little girl.

I embrace you with love,

Elsa

As with her first letter, this cousin seemed to completely deny the
gravity of my mother's situation in life. With an ill husband and
young son, she refused to give in to the reality of my mother's
request for financial help. Notably, she referred to the Easter holiday rather than the Jewish Passover, both of which occur during
the same spring season. Could she have deliberately inserted this to
imply that she had totally assimilated to another culture and could
no longer identify with my mother's religious beliefs? In any case,
it was perfectly clear that my mother's search for familial support
from this relative, one that was the subject back home of countless

stories of having "made it big" in America, had been futile. My mother would never write or attempt to communicate with her wealthy cousins again. She was too busy settling into America by then to pound on unwelcome doors.

Therefore, with no identifiable relatives in the United States to act as our sponsors, we could have been sent to any city or town, but the Jewish Joint Distribution Committee and International Refugee Organization randomly assigned us to this particular western Massachusetts city along the banks of the Connecticut River with a population of about 160,000. Apparently, some members of Springfield's Jewish community had expressed their willingness to take in the refugees, give them a temporary home, and help them ease into the American way of life.

When we arrived at the train station on that July day in 1949, a woman named Sarah Alpert, wearing a stylish shirtwaist dress and a matching snug-fitting hat with a feather on one side, was there to meet us. From my mother's apprehensive appearance and the homemade stone-brown wool coat she wore even though it was July, she must have guessed that we were the mother and child she was expecting.

As we disembarked the train onto the platform, she asked, *Excuse me, ma'am, are you Sidonia Perlstein?*

My mother responded even though she had not understood the exact words:

Yes, I Sidonia.

Your daughter must be tired. Come with me. Mrs. Alpert motioned with her hands. *You'll be staying with me at my home. One of my sons is waiting for us outside.*

My mother held me in her arms as we followed Mrs. Alpert, who carried our suitcase down the long stairway to the main concourse of Union Station and outside. The two of them, Mrs. Alpert and my mother, were both tall, statuesque women with a rather regal bearing. They seemed to complement each other nicely.

We soon pulled up to Mrs. Alpert's three-story Victorian home on Brookline Avenue, one of the nicest streets in the north end of Springfield. Later that day, my mother's Köhler sewing machine arrived and was placed in the bedroom my mother and I were to share.

We are told that you are a very talented seamstress, so I can just imagine how important this sewing machine must be to you. My sons and I look forward to seeing your creations, Mrs. Alpert said with a smile.

With her then limited command of English, my mother could only nod and say, *Yes, tank-a-you very much.*

Before we left Germany, my mother had made sure to indicate to the visa officials that she would not be a public charge in America. She possessed a marketable skill and could make a living as a seamstress. Mrs. Alpert would be the very first person in America to notice my mother's remarkable talent with a needle and thread, but certainly not the last. We had not yet met most of the *grine,* nor anyone else for that matter. The aloneness that my mother felt just then must have been unbearable, but she never showed it to me.

We stayed with Sarah Alpert, who was a widow with two adult sons, for three years, until 1952. During that time, I became a surrogate younger sister for Arnold, a pharmacy student, and Gerald, a private in the U.S. Marines who was fighting in the Korean War for a good portion of the time we lived with them. Our neighbors downstairs, who rented the first floor of Mrs. Alpert's home, were also Holocaust survivors and had arrived in America at around the same time as we had. Their son, Jerry, about seven years my senior, was added to my big brother collection, and their dog, a spitz

The author with Mrs. Alpert in front of her 44 Brookline Avenue home, winter 1952

named Donna, was my playmate even though my mother was hesitant about my playing with dogs. I felt nurtured and accepted by all the inhabitants in that house on Brookline Avenue and wished we would never leave.

It has always been difficult for me to describe my mother adequately. She was not a beautiful woman, but she had a straight back, very dark brown hair, hazel eyes, and she possessed a confident air that made her stand out. She wore no makeup when she first arrived in America but added "Love That Red" lipstick soon after and would wear it as her sole cosmetic during all her ensuing years. Noticeably tight-lipped and stern-faced, she did not reveal much of herself to anyone. I remember her face and stature so well on that day in the winter of 1952 when Mrs. Alpert told us we would have to leave her home. She had decided to marry Sam Greenberg and advised us, *I'll do everything I can to find you another place to live.*

My mother reacted soberly and quietly, while looking over at me, saying, *Ve look for anoder place. Tank you for everyting.*

On the inside, I was unable to react as stoically as my mother had. I was reluctant to leave the Alperts and felt betrayed by everyone, including my mother. I wanted to say, *Let's not leave. Everything I want is here, older brothers, grandparents, and a dog.* But I never verbalized my grief. My mother had trained me well, even at such a young age, to hold all I wanted to say or ask on the inside. So on the outside, I kept quiet, presenting the same deceptively restrained and serious image as my mother did.

By the spring of 1952, when I was just about to turn five years old, we were on our way to Osgood Street, a deteriorating side street only a block or two south of Brookline Avenue, but not nearly as impressive, to meet our destiny with the greenhorns.

CHAPTER 3

The Tattooed Ones

As we settled into our third floor apartment, we heard the sounds of tables being moved, scraping the floor, clanking bottles and glasses, and a flurry of loud voices directly beneath us. My mother, curious about what could be going on, grabbed my hand, and we stepped down the flight of stairs headed for the second floor. At the same time, one of the occupants of the second-floor residence was climbing the stairs to reach our apartment, meeting us midway between the floors. The commotion we had heard was due to preparations for her five-year-old daughter's birthday party, our neighbor told us, and invited us to attend at five o'clock that afternoon.

Looking down at me after the invitation, my mother beamed, *Hanele, ve gonna look da best fun* [from] *everyvon.*

It was our first opportunity to meet a large group of the *grine* all in one place, although I suspect my mother had met some of them while we were still living with the Alperts. Indeed, from the moment of the invitation, my mother's brain was already working to determine what homemade garments we were going to wear. Sure enough, we wore two of our best outfits, full cotton skirts with matching blouses, which my mother had recently stitched on her sewing machine.

The downstairs neighbors' kitchen and living room were set up with numerous tables placed in all parts of the rooms, the space too small to allow them to be end to end. The tables were decked out with paper tablecloths, plastic place settings, and bottles of soda, beer, and whiskey in preparation for a full course meal. Balloons in a variety of colors were suspended from the ceiling along with streams of crepe paper. Bowls of oranges, a delicacy in the part of Europe from which most of them came, stood in the center of each table. Paring knives were stuck in-between the fruit to make eating this newfound sweet easier.

We sat down in two available seats next to the Bach family: William, Gerta, and their two children, Adina, who was my age, and her younger brother, Michael. The mood of everyone there seemed joyful and carefree. Meanwhile, Sally, the birthday honoree, amused everyone with some of her piano tunes. Later, as all the attendees serenaded her, she accompanied them with her best and most practiced piece by far, "Happy Birthday." I wished I could play piano just the way she did.

Mr. Bach, can you pass me da plate of chicken? my mother asked. *My daughter love chicken.* By then, the table was filled with meat, roasted potatoes, pickles, vegetables, and cookies.

Sure, Mrs. Perilshtein, here is some chicken for Chanele. It look good, he said with a broad smile matched by his gleaming eyes, employing the term of endearment for my name that all the *grine* used until I was well into adolescence.

As Mr. Bach reached for the plate, his shirtsleeves rolled up to his elbow, I noticed he had some blue-tinted numbers etched onto the outside of his left forearm. It looked like the numbers 74658, the seven having a horizontal bar across it, so I was not sure whether I was reading it correctly. In my mind, I wondered what those numbers could possibly mean, but for some reason I was not alarmed at all. I just took it in stride, as though there were a lot of things I would never understand about the *grine*.

As I glanced over at the other tables, I noticed that Mrs. Zagruder and Mrs. Stern also bore similar blue-numbered tattoos on their forearms. Although Mrs. Zagruder's was on the inside of her left forearm rather than the outside, it still looked the same as the others. From my experience with the Alperts and observing my mother's arms, I knew not every adult had those numbered forearm tattoos. They had to be singular to this group of people.

Some members of the grine *at one of their parties, around 1952. Sidonia is the fourth woman from the left.*

It was soon after our move to Osgood Street when my mother chose to begin telling her tales about her life growing up in the little village of Dámóc, Hungary, and then her harrowing account of her time as a victim of the Holocaust, emerging as the sole survivor of her family. Often the stories came from a dream she had experienced the night before of life at home with her family or of the horrible events that had taken them all from her. Usually spending her nights toss-ing in her bed, sometimes muttering to herself, she was frequently unable to sleep more than two or three hours a night. Her unrelent-ing insomnia would remain with her for the rest of her life.

Her telling of tales was always a very lopsided endeavor as I rarely spoke during her narratives, giving little feedback and asking few questions. I only listened raptly. I never asked her why many of the *grine* had numbered tattoos on their forearms or why she did not. We never spoke about many things.

Many years later, I learned her prisoner number and that of her sister, Laura, when my mother and I had to select PIN numbers to use the ATM for our joint checking account. When she chose 11105 and then 11106 for me, she soberly advised, *Dat vas mine an Laurie's concentration camp numbers.* Although not tattooed on her arm, the numbers had been permanently seared into her brain. I discovered only through research that she and Laura must have been among the few Hungarian deportees at Auschwitz who were not tattooed owing to the rapid influx of the trains carrying prisoners, sometimes ten to twelve thousand souls a day, to their eventual fate. Although it is probable that the letter "A" preceded the two sisters' serial numbers, my mother had only pointed out the numerical portion.

The date of their arrival at Auschwitz, May 20, 1944, was just a little over two weeks before the D-Day invasion on the beaches of Normandy, which would turn the tide of the war in favor of the Allies. Yet enough time remained for the camp officials to receive almost 440,000 Hungarians in the eight-week period from mid-May to early July 1944 — the last great community of European Jews to meet their cruel destiny in Nazi death chambers during World War II. When the trains carrying the Hungarians finally halted on July 8, 1944, Winston Churchill wrote, "There is no doubt that this is the most horrible crime ever committed in the whole history of the world."

I never talked to anyone about the numerous tattoos I ultimately observed, not even with my childhood friends among the *grine*. As I look back on those days, all of us kids observed quite a bit in our everyday interaction with our parents, but we never discussed our feelings about living with them. Maybe we just could not articulate the appropriate words to describe them or the events that might have shaped them, lacking a noun like *Holocaust*, which was not widely used until the 1970s. Alternatively, we were unable to discuss our parents' behavior or past history because to do so would bring those events too close to reality.

In fact, I knew little about the individual stories of the *grine*, with a few exceptions. I never knew or asked where they came from, what their lives were like before the war, or their feelings about immigrating to a new country. I barely knew their first names. They usually referred to one another formally by their surnames only, such as Mr. Bach, or Mrs. Zagruder, or Mrs. Perlstein. I knew the names of only the very few members of the community who became my mother's close friends. Lately, I have learned their given names for the first time when I read their obituaries in the local newspaper. With each name I read, I instantly see the person's face before me as he or she looked more than fifty years ago, and I try to recall even the slightest memory of our interaction.

The tattoos should have been a sign of many more aspects of my surroundings than I cared to notice at the time. Instead, I was preoccupied with the everyday intrigue and events that continuously unfolded during my time on Osgood Street.

CHAPTER 4

The Matchmaker

Daydreaming has always been a necessary and honorable pastime for me. As a child, I spent many enjoyable hours participating in this imaginative enterprise. My favorite place to daydream was in my bedroom, bereft of furniture except for a donated Hollywood bed, with its white vinyl headboard, and the variously sized cardboard boxes that held my belongings.

I often gazed through my bedroom window at the ancient, dark, ramshackle two-story cedar-sided house right next door whose eaves were on the same level as my room. I cannot remember anyone ever going in or coming out of that decaying house. The activity around the house centered on the numerous pigeons that had made those eaves their home. Nestled on a thick layer of leaves and small branches, they always seemed to be busy bringing dried leaves and twigs from one end of the eave to the other, bolstering their nests. Sometimes I could see the pigeon hens hatching their young and feeding them with the crop milk secreted by both the mother hens and the father cocks. It seemed as though something were always going on up on that roof, a great deal more activity than in my mother's apartment.

While watching those busy birds, I often imagined my mother was a beautiful, vivacious, outgoing woman with whom I had a very open and communicative relationship. We could talk about anything, even some of the painful things that might have occurred to either one of us, unlike our actual, disconnected bond. Having never met him, I was free to imagine my father in the most favorable light. In my daydreams, he was tall, handsome, and charming, an intelligent, cultured man. I knew he wanted the chance to be in my life if he only had known where to find me. It must have been my mother who drove him away, I reasoned, despite his urgent pleas to stay and continue to be present for his daughter.

At a very early age, I sensed we were different from the rest of the *grine*, and the difference was that I did not have a father, but also because my mother and I had never even talked about him or the circumstances of his absence. Other than through my imagination, I knew nothing about him but his name, which I had discovered only because my mother was forced to verbally supply it to the admissions person at Springfield Hospital when I was four to have my tonsils removed. Samuel Yungman was his name.

I noticed in the early years of our stay on Osgood Street that a few bachelors in our community, with neither wife nor children, were sprinkled among the married couples. Although most of them did not fit my ideal of a perfect father figure, if there were an opportunity to acquire a father, it could have been among that group of men, I thought. It was no secret that all of them were looking for wives, as tradition required all Jewish men to possess a spouse and family. Here is how I remember them:

Mr. Messinger was a kind man in his thirties, an age bracket common to most of the *grine*, with gentle, soft eyes and a ready smile. He appeared to be an introvert. I barely ever heard his speaking voice above a quiet whisper. The Landsmans invited him daily to their apartment for breakfast and supper because the poor man had no wife to cook for him. Short in stature, as were many members of the *grine*, he had an overweight bearing that looked even larger than it would on someone just a little taller. Although clean-shaven, he still bore the dark shadow of a beard and mustache to match the dark color of his eyes. Despite his gruff exterior, his mild manner instantly endeared him to me, but I did not think he was really the right match for my mother.

Mr. Zwillen was intimidating. He had a wild temper, which he seemed fond of displaying, allowing me to witness it more than once. His voice was sharp and loud. He lived with his brother and his family in one of the small apartments on Osgood Street. Although he was handsome enough, and a little taller than the rest despite a limp, his hot-headedness gave his face a harsh quality, as though he were constantly sneering. I was afraid of him.

Mr. Stossel was a short man with a thick mustache and horn-rimmed glasses. He had an air of authority and a distinguished gaze. Rumor had it that he had been a university professor in his native land, but his lack of fluency in English and proper credentials forced him to work in a coat factory as a presser. He had a hump on his back, causing him to walk leaning forward and often looking downward. Although he presented himself as Jacob Stossel, I once heard someone refer to him as David, with a different last name. He might have been living under an assumed name. I never knew for sure.

Mr. Goodman was a dignified man. Prematurely gray, he always looked as neat and refined as a gentleman should. He walked with an air of arrogance. People in our community called him the chemist, perhaps an occupation he held in his former country. In America, he worked in a dental laboratory. Sometimes I saw him joining Mr. Messinger for supper at the Landsmans' apartment. I never saw him talk to my mother. In fact, though for a long time I could not figure out why, he seemed to make a point of either turning his head away or looking past us when my mother and I were in the same room with him.

Then there was Mr. Olchinski, the handsomest of the single men. He was a little taller than my mother, perhaps five foot eight, but his slim frame gave the impression of a much taller man. He was fond of telling jokes and laughing at the slightest hint of humor among the others. He had angular, high cheekbones with a strong chin and a full, thick head of brown hair that sometimes fell onto his forehead and covered his perfectly shaped eyebrows. The women, married or not, fawned all over him. I thought he had the potential of becoming a fine father figure for me.

I hoped one of these men, preferably Mr. Olchinski, would ask my mother to marry him and create a new family, including siblings. Yet, nothing could have been further from my mother's mind. She did not seem to care about any of the single men in our community. I never heard her mention any of them by name. She rarely talked with any of them at our numerous gatherings.

Working long hours at the Victoria Dress Corporation as a sewing machine operator, a job she had obtained before we moved to Osgood Street, she did not seem to have the time to think about marriage. At least that was my impression. Sometimes, when I asked her, *Do you think you might ever get married, ma?* she would say, *Oy, Hanele, who vants to cook and clean for a man?*

I wondered whether I could intervene for my mother and capture the attention of some of these men, except Mr. Zwillen, of course, and convince them of my mother's intriguing, clever, and resourceful qualities. If they liked me, they might consider me as a future daughter and change my mother's mind about men and marriage.

I made a point of paying extra attention to these men and sometimes struck up a hapless conversation beginning with something like, *I really like your hair, Mr. Olchinski.*

His reply: *Tanks. It sometimes get in my vay, but I'm glad dat you like it, Hanele.*

Yeah, I really do like it, I sighed.

Dat's really nice, he responded in a somewhat detached manner, with his hands in his pockets and probably hoping

I would soon stop the line of conversation. It was painfully awkward for both of us, but I continued to make these stupid comments for a while, hoping I could ingratiate myself into his heart.

All this started to take place when I was only five or six years old, a time when a child should be thinking about playing hopscotch, grade school events, ballet lessons, or making friends. Worrying about my mother's single status and my responsibility to attract a husband for her and a father for me monopolized both my real and fantasy time. Add to that my mealtime ritual of listening to my mother's terrifying stories of the Holocaust at the kitchen table, and I was turning out to be a rather serious and somber child. My sober personality, combined with my mother's intransigence about the opposite sex, made my pursuit of a father figure seem even more impossible.

CHAPTER 5

Surviving Remnant

Her train did not arrive at Union Station until midnight. The officials had arranged an earlier train from New York City that Saturday, but she preferred to retain her religious beliefs, prohibiting travel on the Sabbath, so she had waited to depart until after sundown. The lateness of the hour, however, did not impede the large contingent that met her at the train station, including many members of the *grine*, the press corps, the mayor of the city, and most important, her sister and brother-in-law, Mr. and Mrs. Puckerman.

The sisters hugged and kissed, tears freely streaming down their cheeks. It was a sight that drew the empathy of everyone who viewed them on the train platform. Someone had brought a bottle of wine, and pouring drinks into plastic cups for some of the entourage, he shouted, *l'chaim*, to life, evoking a round of applause.

During the war, the sisters had been separated as they were being transported from one concentration camp to another. Upon their liberation, they attempted to find each other through the registry of the She'erit Hapletah (the Hebrew term to describe the survivors of the Holocaust after the war, literally, 'surviving remnant') and other locator services, but to no avail.

They had given up all hope that the other one was still alive, until one day, Mrs. Puckerman received a letter from the International Refugee Organization informing her that her sister was alive and interned at a German displaced persons camp. Her screams of joy at hearing the news were so loud that I could hear her all the way from our apartment on the other side of the building. *Oy, Got tsu dank, Got tsu dank, mayn shvester, mayn shvester.* Oh, thank God, thank God, my sister, my sister. She quickly made plans for her sister to come from Germany to Springfield, Massachusetts, to join her family on Osgood Street.

Upon hearing of the impending reunion, the *grine*'s excitement was contagious. They all knew it could just as easily have been one of their own siblings who had been fortuitously located, so they considered it a community event, not confined to just Mrs. Puckerman and her family. They wanted to participate in the welcome party at the train station, and then, at a more private celebration back on Osgood Street.

My mother had attempted similar searches, but not one of her immediate relatives was ever found, only a few cousins from her homeland.

I glad for her, but I vish it vas me, my mother told me when she heard the news of Mrs. Puckerman's good fortune. *It's such a simcha* [an occasion of happiness or joy]. *Sometime people don't understand vhat it's like to lose a sister or broder da vay ve did.*

Yeah, ma. It would have been so nice to find your brother, Dezso. I remember you told me that someone in Auschwitz saw him there on the men's side.

Dat's true, Hanele, but I don't tink he live too long after dat. I vould know.

Maybe, ma. But what if he did survive and he is looking for you?

No, no Hanele. It couldn't happen dat vay, she replied, waving her hand and looking down at the floor.

My mother knew that most of her immediate family, those who were with her at the time of her deportation, had not lived beyond their first day at Auschwitz. Her two oldest sisters, Etel and Szeren, each holding their eight-year-old nephew Mordcha's hand, had been steered to the left along with their father, Simon, ensuring their immediate death in the gas chamber. Her mother, Hani, had passed away from breast cancer a few years before the outbreak of war.

Only she and her sister Laura were selected to go to the right and thereby saved to live for another day. Little Mordcha's father, Dezso, ironically a soldier in the infantry for his home country during World War I, had departed Hungary from a different location, so his fate was much more uncertain. My mother seemed comforted to think that her older brother had not endured the kind of deprivation she and her sister experienced. Still, I always wondered what happened to Dezso after that chance sighting. If he were still alive, maybe my mother would someday have the reunion she so longed for.

My mother was not among them, but twenty members of the *grine* went down to the train station that night to greet Mrs. Puckerman's sister, Mrs. Fryman, and observe the celebratory scene. The local television stations and newspapers all sent their representatives to report on the happy occasion; the mayor showed up to shake the sisters' hands and bring the congratulatory wishes of the city. Things like that did not happen often, and everyone wanted to share in the joyous moment. The newspaper headline the following day in the *Springfield Daily News* read: *DP, REPRIEVED FROM NAZI GAS CHAMBER, REUNITES WITH KIN: Joy at Reaching Springfield and New Home Does Not Erase Marks of Misery from Her Face.*

The following day also revealed a surprise. Mrs. Fryman was not alone. She had brought with her a tall, handsome, yet shy ten-year-old boy, her son Eddie. Torn apart during the war, her other four children and husband were all presumed dead. Somehow, she had found Eddie in the care of a Christian family in The Netherlands, the only other remnant of a family of seven. Finding her sister in America must have been a profoundly emotional surprise as well.

The next night, the *grine* had a party to commemorate the occasion, yet another get-together, when beer, soda, whisky, and food were brought out in the Puckerman's apartment, and the community celebrated late into the night. I was present for only a short time but long enough to notice the tattoo on Mrs. Fryman's forearm, A–23497 — another tattoo to join the markings of so many of my neighbors — and a symbol of the incomprehensible torture she must have endured.

The tattoo was the only overt sign, however, of her unspeakable past. Her hair was a lovely reddish-brown, pulled back into graceful waves that surrounded her neck and outlined an exotic, beautiful face matched by a shapely, slender figure. She spoke little English, so I could not converse with her. However, Eddie, who spoke multiple languages, including English, told me how happy they were to be with family in America.

> *How do you like Springfield?* he asked me.
> *It's okay,* I replied. *I think you'll make friends really fast.*
> *Thank you, I could use some friends. I left mine in Amsterdam.*
> *Don't worry. You'll meet a lot of kids at school here.*

Later, I discovered that Eddie, indeed, did not hesitate to make friends, and, moreover, he was not nearly as shy as he seemed.

Survivor searches for lost family members and friends continued for many years afterward. They continue even today, enhanced by the opening, in 2008, of the International Tracing Service archives at Bad Arolson, Germany, finally revealing the copious

Dezso Perlstein's Buchenwald Prisoner Cards, courtesy of the International Tracing Service and the United States Holocaust Memorial Museum documentation the Nazis kept on all the prisoners they confined during the Holocaust. Fifty million card files were made available through the United States Holocaust Memorial Museum, accounting for more than 17 million victims. It was there that I found data pertaining to my uncle Dezso, among others.

He had, indeed, lived for several months after his sighting at Auschwitz, where he had remained for only ten days before his transfer to the Buchenwald concentration camp, where he was classified as a worker. Nine months after his transfer to Buchenwald as a forced laborer, his condition grew steadily weaker. Separated from his wife and three young children during the previous year, he did not know that they had all been slaughtered. He died, alone, of so-called heart failure at the age of forty-four on February 22, 1945, only a couple months before his potential liberation.

Surely, had any of my mother's siblings or parents lived, they would have been comforted to know that another member of their family had assumed the involuntary role of surviving remnant. Yet, they would also have been saddened to know of the torture she had endured to finally reach freedom and further heartbroken by the lonely, embittered woman she became in America. Despite my wish to make it so, a happy reunion for my mother with one of her siblings never came to pass.

CHAPTER 6

The Broken Angel

When my mother had to leave early in the morning to go to work at the Victoria Dress Corporation or at other times when she had another commitment, she usually left me with one of the *grine*. It was often Mrs. Landsman who invited me into her little apartment and gave me breakfast and her affection. Her son, Yussie, of show time fame, and I grew to be close friends and playmates.

My favorite caregiver, however, was Mrs. Kester. Thinking of her, even today, I am filled with a feeling of warmth and fondness that I have rarely felt for anyone else. My mother always had great difficulty, especially in my early youth, in conveying her sentiments. Her expression always seemed solemn and stiff, as though her emotions were under strict lock and key on the inside. Mrs. Kester, on the other hand, with me, wore her feelings on the outside.

She was a heavyset woman with rosy cheeks and light brown hair with a hint of blond. Her eyes were her most striking feature. They were a gleaming steel blue and always immediately captured my attention. A double strand of fake white pearls often adorned her thick, wide neck. She was married to a prim-and-proper-looking man with a thin, brown mustache whom I never came to know very well. Mr. and Mrs. Kester did not live in the Osgood Street apartment building but in a rented first-floor unit in a two-family house on nearby Dwight Street, within walking distance of our block.

Their only child, Irma, a freckle-faced, chubby girl, was quite brilliant, her nose always inside a book no matter where she was

— floor, sofa, bed, bathroom, eating, or walking down the street. Although I loved books as well, Irma's intellect far surpassed mine along with that of most of us kids. I went over to visit her and asked, *Hey Irma, do you want to play?* She answered, *Sure, I would really like that,* but during most of the time we played, she still would not let go of her book. I often wondered, always seeing her so buried in her reading, why Irma seemed so uncomfortable without a book in her hands.

Mrs. Kester would enchant me with her tales of beautiful fairy princesses who lived in far off lands and attended fancy balls, attracting princes to vie for their affection. Her stories were so fascinating and imaginative, they transported me to a world of beauty and fantasy my mother's stories could never achieve. Most often the princesses she described would coincidentally be named Chana, my own Hebrew name.

> *Yes, Chanele, da beautiful princess vas vaiting in her cestle* [castle] *for da right man to come to marry her.*
> *What was this princess's name, Mrs. Kester?*
> *Vell, I tink da right name for her vas Chana,* she responded using the 'ch' pronunciation of my Hebrew name, beginning with a guttural sound from the throat.

While I was honored that she may have thought of me as a princess, I had an intuition that the name Chana meant more to her than just an eponymous reference to me.

Some children may have known the details of Mrs. Kester's past, but I did not until much later, and I still do not know very much. I remember she continued to struggle with her mental health, seeing doctor after doctor and often sedated into tranquility. In her lucid moments, though, she would still occasionally come to care for me, and I always looked for her if I were visiting her daughter, Irma.

Her presence always seemed to calm me. One time, however, when I was about nine or ten, as I entered through her front door to find my friend, I overheard Mrs. Kester's voice in a phone conversation with her sister, who also lived in our community, speaking of some of her dark secrets.

> *I couldn't sleep last night again. Dose nightmares, I can't stop dem.*
>
> *Ya, I keep seeing my Chanele, mein zise kind* [my sweet child]. *She vas crying so hard and I try to grab her hant, but she fly avay,* she sobbed.
>
> *Ya, I took my pills, but dey don't help me. My bad dreams come anyvay. Oy, vhy did Got take her avay? Vhy?*
>
> *Okay, I vill try to rest. I'm okay.*

I could not help but hear my name, "Chanele." She mentioned my name in reference to her "sweet child." I could only deduce that she must have had another daughter in her homeland, who had lost her life during the war. Mrs. Kester had loved another family before they were snatched from her, a family that haunted her in her dreams, a family she could not let go. She had a new daughter, but she was still haunted by the one she had lost. In that instant, I grew up just a little, with the understanding of why Mrs. Kester was drawn to my name. I suspected that similar circumstances also haunted other members of the *grine*.

She sometimes looked weary and downcast, as though she had just awoken from a deep slumber and was still shaking it off to return to consciousness. Or perhaps she had not slept at all. Her hair occasionally looked oily and stringy as though she had not shampooed it in many days. At other times, she looked happy and alert, ready to take on the everyday tasks of managing a household and participating in the community. Indeed, she seemed to be a study in dichotomies. Still, her unpredictable mood never affected my adoration of her.

I waited for her to come one time when my mother had requested her help in caring for me, but she never arrived. Another member of the *grine*, Mrs. Burman, showed up instead. When I asked what had happened to Mrs. Kester, Mrs. Burman replied, *Oy, nebekh, she is in da hospital. You know, anoder problem mit her kop.* (Oh, poor thing, she has another problem with her head.)

As time went on, I realized Mrs. Kester was still haunted by the relatively recent events that had taken her family and damaged her psyche to such an extent that her sanity hung by a thread. I heard the whispers among the *grine* alluding to more frequent episodes of mental fragility and hospital stays, when poor Mrs. Kester could not come to terms with her horrific past and, therefore, could not manage the daily necessities of her present.

It was difficult for me as a child to understand Mrs. Kester's torment. Even when my mother recounted her own calamitous experiences, she could not convey the full extent of evil and horror she had suffered. So, to me, Mrs. Kester was my angel, broken but nevertheless the embodiment of kindness and compassion.

CHAPTER 7

The Unfortunate Affair

When World War II ended, many individuals, whether survivors of the Holocaust or of other traumatic wartime experiences, found themselves in a strange universe, one totally different from the one they had lived in only a few years earlier. The truths they knew and took for granted for so long were turned upside down, and a whole new set of rules and norms had taken their place.

In this new reality, the survivors had to make decisions that would shape their world for many years to come. Sometimes those decisions should have been delayed or never made at all, given their confusion and vulnerability, yet there was an urgency to move forward with their lives. One of the most important of those decisions was the choice of a mate or spouse.

My mother made one such decision. Since I was ten years old I had known for sure that my father had not disappeared through death. Every year on Yom Kippur, the Jewish Day of Atonement, my mother told me to go down the stairs from the women's section of our little synagogue when it was time to say *Yizkor*, the prayer of remembrance for those who have died. Only those who needed to mourn for a loved one were allowed to stay inside. On my tenth Yom Kippur, when I could say the prayer with proper seriousness, my mother still said, *Go on, Hanele, you can go down da stairs too.* It was then I realized that my father was still alive. There was no need for me to stay in the synagogue to recite the Yiskor prayer.

It took me a long time into my adulthood to discover the real reason for his absence. My mother and father had made an ill-fated choice in a displaced persons camp. They began a relationship they never would have considered before the war, one that resulted in my father disappearing from our lives forever, which altered the course of all our futures.

On Osgood Street, many of the *grine* lived with their own decisions about their spousal selections. They hid their true feelings from the world, yet sometimes, reality would be just too difficult to hide. It was true that some of the couples, like the Posens, a childless couple that often strolled arm in arm on their daily constitutional, had found their soul mates. The Laksers, despite their disparate heights (she exceeding his by half a foot), also seemed emotionally suited.

Some were obviously much less fortunate. Dissatisfied to the point of resentment, Mr. Feldman looked for ways to distance himself from the woman he had met and married after the war, despite their three children. Although Mr. Feldman was as short as the other *grine*, he had handsome features, chiseled cheekbones, dark eyes, and an assertive voice, all of which gave him a commanding appearance. He made friends easily, possessing the knack of displaying a genuine interest in the lives of others. His wife was a former elementary school educator, and though she seemed to be a ditzy, scatter-brained woman, she was learned and articulate. Moreover, she was faithfully devoted to her husband and children.

Mrs. Silverstein was the femme fatale of the *grine*. Although married, with two children, she always looked alluring with bold red lipstick and rouge; long, dark, wavy hair; and low-cut, tight clothing. She was younger than most of the *grine*, a teenage survivor at the end of the war. It was obvious even to a child that many of the men in the community were her admirers.

I imagined that Mr. Feldman and Mrs. Silverstein were characters in one of my mother's favorite television shows, *The*

Loretta Young Show. Ms. Young's pattern of gliding through the door at the start of each show wearing a chic, beautifully fitted evening gown captured my mother's attention as soon as she began to watch American TV. Every week, Loretta featured stories of ordinary people who found themselves in difficult situations. Foreign characters were often portrayed in the title roles attempting to teach the American values of fortitude, resilience, hard work, and the importance of family.

My story line was that these two people fell in love with one another despite their marriages to others. My "TV script" went like this:

Scene 1: *The setting was a group excursion to Forest Park to visit the zoo, enjoy a picnic on the park grounds and a stroll along the beautiful landscape. In those days, the zoo animals were caged in close quarters and had little room to roam. Visitors could get up close to the bars and stand almost eye-to-eye with the monkeys, lions, and polar bears.*

While gazing at the zoo animals, the couple exchanged quiet yet furtive glances. While most of the visitors in the crowd were focused on the animals, Mr. Feldman and Mrs. Silverstein focused on each other, so close that their mouths could have been touching.

Scene 2: *Mr. Feldman stood near the living room sofa wearing only his undershirt and gatkes (undershorts). The sofa was covered with sheets, a pillow, and a blanket. When he was asked why the sofa was made up to look like a bed, he always replied in a sincere voice, "You know, my allergies really boder me vhen I sleep in da bedroom, so I have to come out here to breade [breathe]." It was clear, however, that the air was not much different in the living room than in the bedroom. He was justifying the fact that he was not sleeping with his wife.*

Scene 3: *One day, Mrs. Feldman awoke to find her husband missing. He had not slept in his usual spot on the living room sofa. The sheets were as smooth as the moment she had spread them on top of the seat cushions, the blanket still tucked in on top of them.*

Scene 4: *Soon, their street was abuzz with the news that Mr. Feldman had not slept at home. Someone called his job at the men's suit factory, where he operated a sewing machine, to ask for him, but no one had seen him, and he had not called in sick. Mrs. Silverstein could not be found either. Her husband, known for his volatile temper, was shouting and screaming about how his wife could not be trusted and that he never should have married her.*

Scene 5: *It took another twenty-four hours to find Mr. Feldman and Mrs. Silverstein at the train station downtown. They had been trying to decide whether they could run away together and specifically where they should go, not yet knowing the geography of their new country well. They had slept in each other's arms on a bench at the station and were still debating the pros and cons of slipping away and leaving their families and gave no thought to where they were. No one in their community had called the police since all parties wanted to keep the incident under wraps as long as possible.*

Mr. Feldman's best friend, Mr. Olchinski, who owned a used Chevy, found them. After driving the star-crossed lovers back to their apartment building and escorting them to their respective units, he wondered what repercussions their foiled getaway would bring, concerned that his friend's mistake might cost him his family.

Scene 6: *Mr. Feldman had reddened, puffy cheeks and a bruised lip the following day, and Mr. Silverstein, the femme* *fatale's husband, was slamming doors and rumbling to himself. Yet both Mr. Feldman and Mrs. Silverstein went back to their respective spouses as soon as they returned home, at least outwardly appearing to have left their brief escapade behind them.*

Loretta Young's final word (otherwise known as the moral of the story): *The Feldmans and the Silversteins continued with their marriages because, after all, family was the highest priority.*

Only the occasional snide glance between the spouses in both couples ever betrayed their truce.

CHAPTER 8

The Citizens

By the end of 1954, after having lived in America for five years, following years of study, many members of the *grine* were eligible to take their citizenship examination. They had learned the grammar and vocabulary of the English language, taken instruction in civics about the federal, state, and municipal forms of government and the Constitution of the United States, and began to understand the complexities of American culture.

To prepare for the exam, soon after their arrival in Springfield, they took citizenship classes several nights a week at the nearby Chestnut Street School. It must have been difficult to work every day at their labor-intensive jobs, care for their families, attend night school, and complete the required homework. While it was true that some of them had come from more cultured backgrounds and had attained degrees in a variety of subjects in their native homelands, their inability to converse easily in English and their lack of recognized credentials in the United States had forced them to take entry-level, hard-labor employment to make ends meet.

A number of the men had found jobs at either the Belsky or Kinsler coat factories as pressers, cutters, sewing machine repairers, and tailors. A group of them became peddlers, selling household goods door to door, developing a loyal clientele, and proving that a good salesperson can sell anything, even when he or she does not know the language. Some started saving their earnings in order to buy small farms on the outskirts of Springfield, where they could raise poultry or grow produce. The women searched for work in women's dress factories as sewing machine operators or found jobs as cooks in private schools, like the Lubavitcher Yeshiva, where many of the *grine* kids went to primary school, or on the cooking staff of other institutions.

Mr. Landsman, for example, knew his way around a sewing machine and could sew a coat as efficiently as anyone. Although he was missing a few of his fingers on his right hand, which he often hid in his jacket or pants pocket, his manual dexterity did not seem impaired in any way. His wife, the greatest cook of all, had a pros-thetic eye. (Most of the time, trying to distinguish which eye was the fake one confused me.) They worked at their respective factory and institutional cooking jobs until they could buy their first poul-try farm, which they did by the end of the 1950s.

Sometimes I accompanied one of the children of the men who worked at the coat factories to their father's place of work. Like my mother, the men worked in dark and dingy industrial quarters, cold in the winter and smoldering on the factory floor in the summer. I watched as Mr. Bach, dripping with sweat, operated his steam press, lifting the top layer of the press and plunging it down on each coat, emitting an intense burst of steam with each stroke. At the time, I did not appreciate the strength it must have required to perform this work eight hours a day, five days a week. Yet, Mr. Bach never seemed to complain about his difficult work. I think he viewed it only as a necessary stepping stone to achieving his ultimate objec-tive of someday becoming a prosperous American.

At the Victoria Dress Corporation everyone was stunned at my mother's extraordinary talent. She was as fast and accurate on a sewing machine as anyone they had ever encountered. The owner, Charles Podell, was happy to have her. Yet in the early 1950s, I do not believe my mother had any career goal except sitting behind a sewing machine in that factory. Becoming an American citizen, however, was something she eagerly desired.

As did the others, she went to night school several times a week for almost five years, until she was eligible to take the exam for U.S. citizenship. Starting at the age of two, I often accompanied her. Carrying her familiar brown leather zippered clutch bag containing her texts, she would often peek at her books to check the responsibilities of an American citizen and to look at the reading lessons on the "Basic Principles of the Government of the United States." We would quiz each other about the name of the President of the United States or of the Governor of the Commonwealth of Massachusetts.

By the time she took her exam in November of 1954, when I reached seven years old, we were both steeped in the intricacies of American government. My mother's class notes, tucked inside her books, described the *dudis* of government, the American *revelusen,* and the *constituson as a living dakument.* My favorite note was her warning: *Don't not vote.* She loved every minute of her citizenship training.

When the *grine* began to take the "English for American Citizenship" class soon after their entrance to America, they were assigned to the "basic" course. As an example, my mother arrived in July of 1949, and just three months later, in October, she was already enrolled as a student in the basic class. After completing the requirements of the first course, she graduated to the "intermediate" class the following year. Invited to attend the " 'I Am an American' Night" in March of 1951, she watched as the new citizens that year received their citizenship scrolls while she received a certificate for her studies in Adult Civic Education. It was her first introduction to the ceremonial aspect of earning American citizenship, a forerunner of her own citizenship three years later.

Her memory of the evening, however, focused on meeting the keynote speaker, the former governor, then Sen. Leverett Saltonstall,

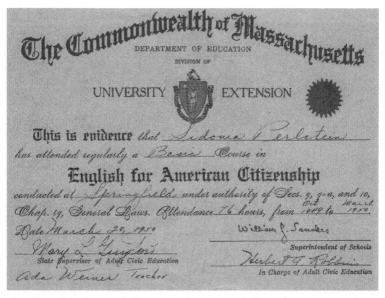

"English for American Citizenship" certificate, Commonwealth of Massachusetts, University Extension, March 20, 1950

a longtime politico familiar to all Massachusetts residents. Always a fan of political celebrities, she gushed, *He look very distingvish but also heymish* [down to earth].

For my mother and her cohorts, becoming a citizen had a psychological effect that far surpassed the elation of a passing grade on an examination. Few natural-born citizens understand the joy that immigrants experience upon becoming United States citizens. The *grine* felt truly honored to be Americans and devoured everything American. They loved American cars, television, restaurants, music, art, free enterprise, the work ethic, Crisco, and Lucille Ball. Like almost all of America, they never missed an episode of *I Love Lucy*. Although my mother and I did not own a television set until later in 1955, I heard the show every Monday night from my bed because the television directly downstairs, in the second-floor apartment, was loud enough for me to hear and absorb every word of the dialogue. I could not wait to someday see the video as well as hear the audio.

The *grine* understood immediately that living in America would be a significant departure from their lives in their native countries. They no longer needed to worry about the pogroms that targeted and persecuted Jews in their little villages or the kind of genocide that removed them from their homes and implemented a "final solution" to rid the earth of all Jews, as demonstrated during the Holocaust. They felt free to pursue their dreams and achieve success in whatever endeavor they chose.

They also were astute enough to know they would need to expand their contact networks and know more about the strategies required to reach their goal of economic success in America. It was after their attainment of citizenship that the *grine* began to develop their acumen in navigating the American way of life and spent the rest of the 1950s preparing for their moves up the economic ladder.

The January 28, 1955, edition of the *Jewish Weekly News* reported: *Club Hatikvah is planning a citizenship party on Saturday night, February 12, at the Jewish Community Center. The large number of Hatikvah members who recently received American citizenship will be honored. State Representative Phillip Kimball will be the main speaker. Miss Tilly Steinhardt will play her popular piano tunes.*

Club Hatikvah was established in the early 1950s, only a few years after the arrival of the *grine*. It held larger gatherings in a rented hall and was slated to sponsor the celebration in honor of the momentous occasion of citizenship. *Vill you be dere, Mrs. Perilshtine?* asked Mr. Messinger.

Dere vill be dancing music, he added with a little lilt in his voice.

Yeh, I tink I vill go if I can find somebody to take care on Hanele, I heard my mother respond in a nonchalant manner. *Den I vill see you dere.*

That exchange was the closest I ever saw my mother come to responding positively to a man's obvious overture. And it was not even an invitation for a date. Citizenship had changed her. She may have been a depressed, lonely woman, living a life as a single working mother with a small child, but she had developed a much more assured manner, proud of her American status and steeped in American culture. Becoming a citizen made her more confident in her ability to manage our lives without any assistance from a man. I guess, in a way, my mother's citizenship was a mixed blessing, viewed in regard to my dreams for her future marital bliss.

CHAPTER 9

The Club

Club Hatikvah, named after the Hebrew word for hope, was more than just a vehicle for parties and celebrations. It became a way of alleviating isolation and offering social support to all the members of our immigrant community. Many joined shortly after the club's formation, and some became long-term officers and leaders of the organization. The old Park Manor on Fort Pleasant Avenue in Springfield was often chosen as a meeting place for events that included food, music, dancing, and mixing.

In 1954, the *Jewish Weekly News* announced one of Hatikvah's early events: *PLANS FOR A PURIM PARTY: The Hatikvah Club will have its annual Purim Party at Blake's Restaurant on Saturday evening at 8 pm. Music and dancing from 8-12 pm featuring John Tranconi and his band. Dancer Joni King will be the guest performer. Buffet refreshments will be served at midnight.* Then a list of the names of the party committee followed, including that of the president of the Women's Auxiliary, Mrs. Landsman.

Purim, one of the most festive of Jewish holidays, celebrates the deliverance of the Jews from a king whose aide, Haman, plots against them. A beautiful woman, Esther, hides her Jewish identity and attracts the eye of the king to become his new queen, replacing the previous queen, Vashti, who had refused to publicly display her beauty, thus disobeying the king's command. Esther convinces the king to save the Jews from the wrath of Haman. The villain, Haman, and his plot to annihilate the Jews are thereby ultimately destroyed. The holiday is one traditionally of merriment and charity, when Jews dress in costumes portraying characters from the Purim story or, in contemporary times, in any costume they wish. Donations to worthy charities are usually offered as well. The *grine's* desire to host a party in honor of Purim, when enjoyment and high spirits are paramount, seemed appropriate.

Most of the members of Hatikvah were couples who often shared the Polish language in addition to Yiddish and enjoyed a good game of cards. When I think of the club members in those days, I often picture them sitting at card tables, four at a table, dragging on their cigarettes and playing for nickel bets. Sometimes I could hear a pin drop for what seemed like an eternity until the next player made a wager or played his or her card. Since my mother refused to play, I never knew the names or rules of the games, but I understood they were intense.

The card players seemed to be a private group, and when my mother would not participate, it only enhanced my feelings of exclusion. Although my mother once told me her family in Hungary were expert domino players and that she used to love strategizing and engaging in lengthy games in her youth, those days seemed far in the past. Games were too trivial to be part of her life in Springfield. *I not interested in playing such games*, she said. Her attitude served only to set us further apart from the rest of our community.

The children of the *grine*, like me, often accompanied their parents to Club Hatikvah events. I loved the joyous atmosphere and the opportunity to sing and dance with my friends. My mother and I may have attended the Purim party the year before, but only the new adult citizens were invited to the citizenship celebration. So I stayed home that night in 1955, with Mrs. Kester.

When my mother returned home that particular night, I knew something awful had happened to her. She was sitting hunched over at the kitchen table, her head cupped in both her hands, talking to herself in a low voice.

What's the matter, ma? Did something bad happen tonight?
I asked, lightly touching her hand.

At first she responded, *I okay, Hanele. I fine.* But when I questioned her further, she finally looked up at me and slowly said, *Somevon call me a name. Some jerk call me a name.*

My mother never used the term *jerk* lightly. To her, it was one of the most serious words in the English language, used to describe someone in the most adverse manner possible. Several years later in my adolescence, in a rare moment of reverie, I heard her use the same word to describe my father.

I learned that one of the wife seekers, the one whom I most feared, had asked her to dance. She had politely refused. Mr. Zwillin had fancied he might be the one to become my mother's beau when no one else seemed to succeed. Her refusal roused his tempestuous nature to such an extent he went into a tirade and shouted epithets at her, questioning her moral character, for deigning to refuse his advances. All this occurred in front of the *grine* community, where everyone could observe the scene, buzz about it for several days, and also keep it in their minds for some time to come.

She requested a ride home from the celebration and never attended a Club Hatikvah event again. I realized, even as an eight-year-old, that the incident had served only to harden her heart even more severely against any meaningful relationship with the opposite sex. Not that it mattered, but I never knew whether she ever danced with Mr. Messinger.

CHAPTER 10

The Shul

We called it the Russische Shul, the Russian synagogue, in honor of the Russian and Eastern European Jews who had laid its cornerstone in 1923 and completed construction the next year, twenty-five years before our arrival on American soil. Bearing a large Star of David embedded in cement at its apex in front of the brick structure, its actual name was Congregation B'nai Israel (Sons of Israel), but none of us kids knew its real name throughout our childhood. Referring to it as the Russische shul seemed to infer a link to our parents' orthodox shuls before they came to America and gave the community a feeling of kinship and unity.

A larger, more majestic orthodox synagogue, known simply as the Big Shul, a massive brick building set far back from the street, its walkway lined by thick green hedges and built around the same time, stood less than a mile away on Chestnut Street. Yet most of the members of our little refugee enclave preferred the diminutive, close-knit surroundings of the Russische Shul. Not knowing any of its members, we used to say the Big Shul was only for snobs, too grandiose for down-to-earth, unassuming people like us.

Located on Dwight Street, just a little farther north from our apartment, easily within walking distance, the shul was the center of our religious and often social activity. Stemming from the High German word for "school," the Yiddish word *shul* reflects one of the goals of any synagogue, to act as a focal point of Jewish education

The old Russische Shul, now Daniel's New Bethel Church of God in Christ, painted white, Star of David at the top, 2006

and social consciousness as well as prayer. Combined with my early studies at the Lubavitcher Yeshiva, our shul was an extension of my development in Jewish religion, tradition, and culture.

Curiously, my mother and I were not committed to Jewish laws and commandments. We purchased kosher meat at Chernick's Kosher Market in our neighborhood and did not mix meat with dairy as our religion's law demanded, but I think the practice came more from my mother's family history in her homeland, growing up in a strictly Orthodox home, than from any devotion to her faith. We almost never attended the shul on the holiest of all days, Shabbos, the Sabbath, usually reserving our attendance for holidays, like Rosh Hashanah, the Jewish New Year, or Yom Kippur, the Day of Atonement, the most important holy day and fast day on the Hebrew calendar.

Before the scheduled start of the service, the *grine* and other members of the congregation usually gathered outside along the sidewalk at the bottom of the five stairs leading up to the synagogue doors to greet and wish one another a *gut yontif*, a good holiday. People used the occasion to catch up on the latest news about family members and to express their concern about a loved one's illness. *Du solst blaybn gezint* (You should stay well) was a wish among them for the coming Hebrew year. The shul was the place I remember where most of the *grine* met as a group, dressed in their finest garments, and, with their children in tow, celebrated their Jewishness.

As we entered the building, my mother grabbed my hand and said, *Come mit me, Hanele. Let's go upstairs an find our seats on da right side of da voman's* [her pronunciation of "women's," rejecting the plural] *section. You know, vhere ve alvays sit.*

In this orthodox congregation, only men were allowed to fully participate in the service and, therefore, possessed the right to sit downstairs to face the Holy Ark, which housed the Torah. Tradition had it that the distraction of members of the opposite gender would impede the men's full focus on the prayers of the day, so women were relegated to separate worship on the upper floor.

> *Okay, ma. Oh, I see Mrs. Posen is sitting near us,* I replied. Knowing that Mrs. Posen was a Jewish scholar, I leaned over to her as we sat down and whispered: *Hello, Mrs. Posen. You know, I learned about the Prophet Isaiah at school this week. I think we'll be reading a portion from the Book of Isaiah today.*
>
> *Ya, Hanele. You are right,* Mrs. Posen said. *It is very inspiring.*
>
> *Sha, Hanele! Don't talk right now,* my mother admonished, clearly annoyed by my chatter.
>
> *Sorry, ma. Just talking about Isaiah,* I said, as I looked at Mrs. Posen, who put her index finger to her mouth in

acknowledgment of my mother's request for silence.

Can't you see dis is a place for praying? Dere is no talking in shul, my mother reprimanded again, with her most serious expression.

She could be rigid and demanding in that way, and when she was, I knew better than to disobey her. She had her strict set of expectations, and I was tacitly bound to abide by them.

It was only on those holidays in shul when I witnessed my mother reaching out for any semblance of spirituality, reading her siddur, the prayer book, mouthing the Hebrew words, and intently observing the service down below in the men's section. I wondered whether her intensity at those moments when we were praying in the synagogue represented her way of paying homage to her lost family, which had uttered the same Hebrew words and prayed the same Hebrew prayers. She seemed unable to capture the same spiritual fervor at home. I never saw her in prayer, aside from lighting the candles on Friday night, the eve of Shabbos, or mention God outside of the synagogue. If participating in the Hebrew prayers in the synagogue was the only way that she could make a spiritual connection with her family, why did she attend services so infrequently?

Down below in the main section of the sanctuary where the men sat, it looked like a sea of suits covered in part by *tallit* (prayer shawls) draped like white scarves around their shoulders and upper arms. Our view captured the top of the men's heads, where their yarmulkes were perched, each bending over to read their *siddur* or *chumash* (the printed book of the Torah), some enthralled in prayer and some busy in conversation with their neighbors. I always searched for Mr. Olchinski's shock of thick brown hair under his yarmulke so I could focus on him as he prayed. Sometimes I noticed him looking up toward the women's section, seemingly searching for someone to meet his gaze, but he never seemed to target any woman specifically. When I observed him looking up, I made sure to divert my stare in another direction quickly so he would not detect my gawking.

Up on the *bima*, the raised floor or platform, stood the rabbi and cantor, men whose oversized tallit were folded over several times along their shoulders, serving to intensify their prominence. The cantor's full-throated tenor voice rose high over our heads, leading the congregation in singing the holiday prayers. His voice seemingly soared well beyond the dome above us and headed directly for the heavens. Sometimes I saw my mother close her eyes as the cantor chanted the liturgy, his melody inspiring her remembrances of the siblings and parents she had joined in prayer on the Sabbath and holidays when she was young.

One activity always seemed incongruous to me in a house of prayer, and for a long time, I was unsure of its purpose or intent. It was an auction. On holidays, before the Torah was taken out of the Ark to begin the Torah service, the cantor would speak in Yiddish to the men in the congregation in what seemed like a secret code. He spoke so sharply and rapidly, I could barely make out the words, which reminded me of the snappy cadence of an auctioneer I had seen on television.

After he had spoken a few words, a man would raise his hand and respond with a one- or two-word reply, like *eyn hundert* (one hundred). The cantor would then point to the respondent and repeat *eyn hundert*. Another raised hand followed and someone quietly stated, *hundert un tsvantsik* (hundred and twenty). The numbers grew increasingly higher until no more bids ensued, when the cantor stopped and announced the highest bidder for the first item to be auctioned.

This scene went on in a highly entertaining manner, with each bid in quick succession until the cantor had completed the auction of all the intended items. A contented smile on his face, he announced the end of the auction, aware that he had raised a tidy sum to aid in filling the synagogue's oil tank for the winter.

It took me a while to determine what items were auctioned off on the High Holy Days, but I discovered they were all the same thing — the honor of coming up to the bima and reciting an *aliyah* (meaning an ascent or a going up), a blessing at the Torah during each portion read at the service — six of them on Yom Kippur, unless it was the Sabbath, when it was seven. While normal business transactions were forbidden on the Sabbath and holidays, an aliyah was no normal business activity. Bidding for the honor and privilege of elevating the soul by representing the congregation before the Torah was not the purchase of a tangible item. It was the pure gift of an opportunity to participate in a spiritual elevation to which all Jews aspired. What seemed to me an entertaining interlude during the morning service was actually an introduction to a sacred ritual connecting the congregation to previous generations and to God. Yet it is the auction itself that I remember the most.

When it came time to blow the *shofar,* the ram's horn, used, among many other reasons, to call the congregation to its spiritual work and to arouse God's compassion, especially important during the repentant period of the High Holy Days, I was always curious as to who would be chosen to blow the long blast to end the Yom Kippur holiday. On Rosh Hashanah, the shofar was blasted one hundred times with sounds of varying lengths, but on Yom Kippur, one long blast announced the end of the Day of Atonement, usually just around dusk. Often the cantor was the one to blow the shofar, with a strength surpassing that of any trumpet player.

However, when I was ten years old, little Mr. Stossel, with his humped back and his horn-rimmed glasses, was the one who took on the task. He quietly stepped up to the bima, holding a shofar that was longer and more twisted than any I had ever seen. If he had held it vertically, the shofar would have been equivalent to one half of his whole body, or so it seemed. An instrument of that size would have required a powerful and skillful breath to elicit a strong sound, which I doubted Mr. Stossel possessed.

> *Oh no, ma! Mr. Stossel is going to blow the shofar. That thing is just too big for him. Oh, no!*
>
> *Don't vorry, Hanele. Vhy vould he go up on da bima if he couldn't do it? He is not dat stupid. Just vatch.*
>
> *I can't watch, ma,* I said, turning my head around. *He should never have agreed to blow the shofar!*
>
> Indeed, contrary to my prediction, he proceeded to blow the horn so loudly and clearly that he achieved a sound whose force could easily have been heard outside the building and roused a thousand angels. The blare of the shofar must have lasted twenty seconds. I turned my head back half way around, shocked, my mouth hanging wide open.
>
> *How did Mr. Stossel do that, ma? I didn't think he would be able to push a sound like that out of the horn.*
>
> *It take a lot of practice, mayn leben* ['my life,' a term of endearment she used for me]. *He must be practicing for a long time.*
>
> *Who would have known?* I shrugged.

The mystery of Mr. Stossel seemed to have no end.

As we remained in the synagogue all day during Yom Kippur, it required a good deal of stamina. By late afternoon, after a full day involving much sitting, standing, intense prayer, striking of the heart while asking God's forgiveness for the previous year's sins and transgressions *(I abuse, I betray, I am cruel . . .),* and fasting from food and drink beginning the previous evening at sundown, some of the adults became dehydrated and lightheaded. Children were exempt from the fasting requirement, so I remained alert to all the events of the day, like the memorable fainting spells.

Ma, that's Mrs. Lorey. She just dropped down to the floor! I saw it all happen, I shouted at my mother, pointing to the opposite end of the women's floor while everyone around us gasped.

Oy, Hanele. Nebekh [poor thing], *she look very pale,* my mother replied, after turning to look in Mrs. Lorey's direction.

Before we knew it, someone had already rushed to Mrs. Lorey's aid, positioning the smelling salts below her nostrils, quickly reviving her, raising her up, and rushing her down the stairs and out of the building to breathe in the brisk autumn air. A few minutes later, we heard a cry down below us, and all the women crowded around the railing, their eyes searching for the source.

Do you think it's someone we know who just fainted downstairs, ma? I asked, furtively taking in the full scope of the men's section to see whether it might be Mr. Olchinski.

Ve vill know in a few second. I'm sure dey vill help him be all right, Hanele. Don't vorry.

Another fainting incident had indeed occurred, this time downstairs in the men's section. Again, the smelling salts were quickly produced, bringing the man back to consciousness. As I watched a group of congregants pick up the woozy man and rush him out of the synagogue, I kept my relief that it was not Mr. Olchinski to myself.

Recollecting these incidents that occurred in my shul, I cannot remember a Yom Kippur at the Russische Shul when the same dramatic fainting away did not occur and, in turn, the smelling salts did not come into play. However, my mother was never one of those whose fasting caused her to suffer the effects of dehydration. She would never have allowed herself to be the victim of a day of deprivation, always keeping up her strong persona. Interestingly, although the fainting spells I witnessed in my youth were memorable, I have never observed one since.

It was on the festive holiday of Simchat Torah (Rejoicing of the Torah), however, that I recall some of my happiest moments at our shul. Celebrating the juncture when the annual reading cycle of the Torah is completed and begun anew, Simchat Torah was a time when both adults and children discarded their inhibitions in the house of prayer and sang and danced around the sanctuary downstairs and the small lobby in front as though all their cares were forgotten. Women came down from their usual upstairs section of the sanctuary to the main level and danced and celebrated along with the men, although still separately. The men embraced the synagogue's Torahs as though hugging a newborn infant, jubilantly dancing with them to Hebrew tunes sung by the congregation.

Children held small flags bearing the Star of David, recently adopted as the flag of the new State of Israel, an apple impaled onto the top of the pole extending above the banner. They marched around for hours with their flags, laughing at one another and enjoying the general gaiety of the occasion. Usually a sober, solemn venue, our shul turned into a spirited house of merriment on Simchat Torah. Afterward, as we walked home, we ate our apples — core, seeds, and all.

For all the intensity and spirituality I observed at our shul, I rarely saw the same devotion to Jewish ritual and prayer among the *grine* on Osgood Street. Some of them had totally abandoned adherence to *kashrut*, the dietary laws, and never attended our synagogue on the Sabbath or for daily prayers. A few of the men donned their *tefillin*, the morning ritual of tying phylacteries, two small boxes containing prayers on parchment paper inside, attached to leather straps wrapped around the head and left arm, hand, and middle finger. This daily ritual represented devotion to the meaning of the holiest of Jewish prayers, the *Shemah*, which states the unity of one God. It seemed like most of the men abandoned the ritual, possessing an aversion to revisiting the religious customs they had routinely practiced before coming to America.

I wondered whether they had abandoned their religious devotion because of their perceived betrayal by a God who had promised his aid and protection if only they followed his commandments. Following his commandments had offered no reprieve from the brutality and losses they had experienced. Where was God when his people needed him the most? Indeed, I believe my mother was among this group of disenchanted men and women, and I have absorbed her skepticism.

Yet, the words of the Lord in chapter 58 of the Book of Isaiah, the passage we read on the fast day of Yom Kippur, in which he describes the proper manner of fasting, have remained with me throughout the years and shaped much of my life's work. *The Jewish Study Bible: Jewish Publication Society Tanakh Translation* reads:

No, this is the fast I desire:
To unlock fetters of wickedness,
And to untie the cords of the yoke,
To let the oppressed go free;
To break off every yoke.
It is to share your bread with the hungry,
And to take the wretched poor into your home;
When you see the naked, to clothe him,
And to not ignore your own kin.
Then shall your light burst through like the dawn.

CHAPTER 11

Faithful Friends

Although my mother was unable or unwilling to immerse herself fully among the *grine*, she seemed to have a great affinity for individuals she had met in a displaced persons camp after the war. She must have felt they had witnessed some of the events that had transformed her life and understood her emotions better than anyone else ever could. She was probably right.

In 1998, after discovering some of my mother's letters and photographs during her move to elderly housing, I finally learned some of the secrets she had tried so hard to keep from me throughout my life. As I gazed at one picture of a young man and woman sitting side by side, their heads slightly tilted toward each other, I turned the photograph over to read the inscription on the back in Yiddish. It identified their location as the "Bergen Belsen Camp" and indicated the date, June 6, 1947, a time when my mother was more than six months pregnant. In a confusion of singular and plural, the duo referred to themselves as my mother's "faithful brothers and good friend." Their faces reminded me vaguely of the couple my mother and I had visited in 1952 when I was just five years old, two years before my mother became a citizen. She had taken a week off from her new job at the dress factory to take the long train ride from western Massachusetts to Montreal, Canada, to see them.

The strength of their relationship and my mother's commitment to aiding others with whom she shared a firm bond were displayed first in the following letter, which preceded our trip, written in simple Yiddish with a little Hungarian flair, using the Latin instead of the Hebrew alphabet:

February 20, 1950   Zarnuga, Rehovot [Israel]

In God's name

Dearest Sidi and Hanele — May you prosper!
May you live to be 120, Amen!

You should forgive us, that we have been delayed in writing, for you know, of course, we received the furniture from Felix, and we wanted to pick it up. But unfortunately it is impossible for us, because they wanted a lot of money from us, that is, for customs and luxury taxes. And so we have been occupied and unfortunately we haven't accomplished anything. But we hope that we will pick it up as quickly as possible because we are both working. . . on an apartment. It is true that it is very difficult, but what can we do about it? Believe me, we are not happy at all, because unfortunately it come to naught here, because when you have . . . all the furniture to give away, it would be very easy for us. But this way, believe me, the devil should take it. I write this from deep in my heart.

In that you write that you gave us nylon stockings for Eva. Believe us that this pleases us very much that you are sending them. . . . You should not do that, because you are also a newcomer, because we know how it looks. And we ask you to take care to follow up on what you wrote, that you will send us a picture of Hanele . . . because we are already very curious. I hope that in the letter you will write, that you will remember to include a picture. . . . We are with the help of God in the best of health, which we also hope to hear from you.

We are sending you the address for Moyshele, which you requested of us. In the meanwhile, he hasn't written to us, which we requested from the boys, because they always fail to. They sent us the address for the boys. It has been a long time since we received any correspondence from them. What that is all about, I don't know. I only hope they will write shortly. . . .

Felix is certainly already in America because he already wrote us from Wentorf [transit camp], *and he has traveled by airplane because he writes that it worked out with his first embarkation by train. . . . We haven't received any correspondence from America. . . . We are still waiting every day.*

Write to us about what you are up to and what the child is doing. . . . You wrote us that you sent us a package of old things. It is true that everything comes mostly very well, and I understand that you are definitely going to send us something. I only ask that you shouldn't go out of your way, because we cannot understand how you can do it because you write that you aren't working. If you were working, we could understand, but otherwise, I can't understand.

Write to us and tell us about everything that is going on with you. I'll end here. We send you greetings and kisses. We especially send Hanele many kisses from us, your faithful friend Jozsi.

This is Eva writing.

I don't have much to write. Jozsi already wrote everything. Special greetings and many kisses and many special kisses for Hanele, many thousand times from me. Your friend who hasn't forgotten you and who thinks and speaks of you often. Please answer right away.

Eva

Then, at the end of the following year, this next letter arrived from my mother's "faithful friends" as they were about to emigrate:

December 4, 1951 Rehovot

Dearest Sidike and Hanele,

You are probably cross with us that we haven't written you until now, as you certainly know how a person can be at a time like this, when we [have so much to do] for such a [trip], only thank God we have fulfilled our goal with God's help. So, Sidike, we hope to have the tickets this month on December 17ᵗʰ. We have taken care of things, so that we have done everything. Sidike, we thank you heartily for the package, which we received from you. Everything arrived in the best of condition as we have written. We hope to happily repay you because it is gone very well with us. . . . Really, we are very thankful to you for all that you have . . . even having sent money . . . but thanks to God we . . . [will receive] everything, and then I will send you the letter. I will send you two papers because maybe you need one to go to court [or some other legal proceeding]. Then you will have one in hand.

And now, Sidike, you don't need to write to me — only until such time that we don't write to you, because we will arrive in Paris. We will write you immediately first and foremost. I will end my writing. Be healthy, greetings and kisses from your Eva who hasn't forgotten you.

Jozsi and Eva

These letters indicate that the husband and wife probably immigrated to Israel in 1949 or 1950 and lived in an "absorption camp," where life was distinctly harsh and austere. To accommodate the large influx of Holocaust survivors, Eastern Europeans, and later displaced Middle Eastern residents all wishing to gain entrance to the British Mandate for Palestine and then the new State of Israel after the war, temporary camps were erected to house the immigrants until they could be mainstreamed into Israeli society. Although originally constructed as tent camps, most likely by the time this couple arrived, they had been converted to more substantial transitional housing made of tin. Lacking relatives or other forms of sponsorship, Jozsi and Eva faced, in reality, yet another displaced persons camp after the one they had left in Germany. Their frustration with their living conditions was evident.

Additionally, some curious references appear in the first letter pertaining to "Moyshele . . . and the boys." Since Jozsi and Eva were with my mother when she became pregnant at the displaced persons camp, it is almost certain they were familiar with my father and the circumstances involved in my birth. I suspected "the boys" might have been a reference to my father and one of his young relatives, maybe a brother. My mother apparently requested the address of "Moyshele," who seemed to have a direct connection to the boys. She may have been seeking their location in order to send them a message about the child they had in common.

In the second letter, written as these friends were about to emigrate, further mystery appears in a reference to "two papers because maybe you will need one to go to court." These words called to mind the letter I had found among my mother's papers, which she purportedly wrote in 1952 to a chief rabbi from her homeland, asking for corroboration of a meeting that occurred at the Bergen Belsen displaced persons camp between my mother and father in 1948 about their baby's future welfare. In that letter, my mother wrote of "legalization proceedings" to legalize my paternity. Could she have asked for some kind of documentation from Jozsi and Eva to use in these "proceedings" as well? However, if such proceedings ever occurred, their results remain unknown to me.

Both letters close with the Yiddish phrase *dain nist fergesene fraindin* [sic] (your friend who has not forgotten you). It was still clear, though, that their kind of friendship seemed to be a departure from the cautious relationships my mother developed with her new friends and acquaintances in America. The *grine* were not with her right after the war, when she made some of her impulsive decisions upon finding herself alone in a displaced persons camp. By the time she immigrated to Springfield, she had already been through three concentration camps, lost her whole family, spent four years in a displaced persons camp, and gave birth to a child.

Jozsi and Eva knew what my mother had endured more than anyone. Knowing there was nothing she could hide from them, she may have felt emotionally liberated, allowing her to create a genuine connection. Concerned about their welfare in primitive surroundings while still in a transition camp, she had sent them packages of clothing, money, and other staple items until they could become permanently settled, even though she was a "newcomer" and did not have much herself. She did not care about any suspicion she may have aroused as a newly arrived immigrant sending care packages to others in need. Looking forward to seeing her true friends again, she was willing to take a week off without pay, seek permission as an alien to leave the country, and to spend the little money she possessed to purchase train tickets to Canada.

As a child, I wondered whether other members of my community also had friends they had left in displaced persons camps or their homelands. Surely this must have been the case for each one of them. Yet they seemed to all get along so well with one another, without much difficulty in forming solid friendships. Not like the struggle my mother had in forming new bonds in her adopted homeland.

As time went on, Jozsi and Eva eventually moved again, this time to the West Coast. My mother rarely saw them, but she spoke of them often and never forgot her "faithful friends." I just wish she could have made similar faithful friends in America.

CHAPTER 12

The Lucky One

Depending on the time and place, I have perceived the facts surrounding my birth from two opposing perspectives. Simply put, sometimes I have considered my birth to a single-parent Holocaust survivor as good luck and at other times grossly unfortunate. Which perspective was stronger on any given day depended on my mood, events, observations, and what people said to me about my bastard status. Here is what I mean:

On Osgood Street, I spent many hours playing with Adina Bach. She always seemed level-headed, composed, and more developmentally mature than I was, and I was proud to be her friend. We often played yo-yo, hopscotch, read *Betty and Veronica* comic books, or listened to records. However, I realized that Adina's parents placed adult responsibilities on her regarding housekeeping and specific chores.

In contrast, I had few housekeeping requirements or special chores. My main responsibilities, starting at a very early age, revolved around being a good student and acting as the model for my mother's creative fashions. I knew my mother expected me to do the job well, but she rarely disciplined me when I disappointed her — if I don't count the pointed stare. Instead, she seemed incessantly sad. Ensuring my mother's happiness was my foremost duty.

Adina's home environment, however, was marked by high expectations matched by severe consequences if they were not met.

When Adina had not completed her housekeeping chores, like polishing the family silver by the time her father returned home, she faced harsh punishment. Her father did not seem to care whether anyone, such as me, was watching as he applied his cruel discipline, so I witnessed it more than once. He took off his belt and pushed his daughter to the floor on her back and proceeded to whip her, particularly around the most tender part of her legs, her inner thighs, until they were red and bleeding, while he shouted at her about her supposed negligence and the shirking of her responsibilities.

When he finished, he walked away, leaving her on the floor to cry. I was heartsick at what I had witnessed, but never spoke about it with Adina. I was too afraid of getting between a father and a daughter and possibly facing the same punishment from him. I just helped her to rise from the floor and went into the bathroom with her to help apply a wet washcloth to her stinging wounds. A few days later, Adina would say to me, *You're lucky you don't have a father. That's for sure. I wish I didn't.* I could not reply, because, at that moment, I did feel very lucky. If fathers inflicted corporal punishment on their children, I certainly did not want one.

Then there was the time I played with Mrs. Kester's daughter, Irma, the bookworm. Often our activity entailed just walking down Dwight Street. All I can remember is always trying to distract Irma from the book she happened to be reading when I first entered her house, which was no easy task. Although I admired her intellect, perhaps I did not convey that to her. Wearing my mother's fashions, I may have seemed like someone who displayed a supercilious attitude toward her.

One day, when we were about ten years old, we took one of our frequent walks. She seemed to be depressed and angry at the world that day. I never fully realized how difficult it must have been for her to live in a household with an emotionally unstable mother and a pedantic, distant father, relying mainly on her books for sustenance.

I could have been the convenient person before whom she could release her pent-up emotions. Attempting to find an upside to her life, she began a contest of "who is better than whom."

She was smarter. I was skinnier. She had better grades in school. I had more friends. She read more books. I read more comic books. Then she blurted out what was really on her mind, the detail that could not be disputed: *I have a father and you don't.*

I was stunned at her blunt statement. No one had ever said that to me before, so her boldness left me speechless. None of the *grine* or their children had ever verbalized their thoughts about my mother and my circumstances, at least not to me, perhaps fearful of hurting me. Other than Adina envying me for my lack of a paternal figure who might physically harm me as hers did, no one had ever approached me about it. I made a habit of never bringing up the subject of my father, never even saying the word *father* if I could help it. I began to weep uncontrollably at Irma's outburst and quickly lost the feeling in my arms and legs. I asked to go back into Irma's house to call my mother and beg her to come to retrieve me since I was too numb to walk back home alone.

When my mother arrived, I explained, through my sobbing, what Irma had just asserted. Without initially saying a word to either me or to Irma, whose presence I barely noticed, except for hearing her wretched sobs as a backdrop to my own, my mother put her arms around me. *Come, Hanele, let's just go. Ve don't have to say anyting.* She comforted me, as I just looked at her, unable to talk anymore. We walked the block or so back to our apartment building. I had never felt as unlucky as I did after Irma's vindictive outburst. Everyone around me had a father but me, and perhaps they were talking about me behind my back.

Years later, I still vividly remembered this scene, but I viewed it from a totally different standpoint. Yes, Irma had a father, although detached, one who left her lonely and lacking in self-confidence, as well as a mentally fragile mother. Indeed, each of the children of the *grine* had to cope with the legacy of their parents' survival and deal with the consequences on their own terms. Just as Irma did, all of us were forced to find our own distinct coping mechanisms to deal with our parents, damaged in some ways by their past subjection to inhumane forces.

The most important player in this drama, I realize now, was my mother. How did she feel about what Irma had said to me? How was she able to keep her composure in calming her devastated daughter? To calm me, she had remarkably summoned all her resilience and strength, without giving away any of the inner turmoil she must have experienced.

CHAPTER 13

Yuri's Story

Where did my mother learn resilience? For that matter, where did any of the members of my community learn their remarkable resilience? Was it an innate characteristic or had they learned it from another source, from their parents and siblings during their childhoods or from someone in their wartime experiences?

The main character in one of my mother's numerous dinnertime stories could have been the model for her toughness. She relayed this story, as she had all the others, with a steady gaze and a firm voice, with no hint of emotion or vulnerability. I have always referred to it as Yuri's story.

While interned at the Bergen Belsen concentration camp, my mother became well acquainted with her Blockälteste (block leader), a woman named Yuri. By the time my mother had reached the camp, having departed from Dachau, it was already December 1944, the start of a particularly ferocious winter. Yuri was the first person to greet my mother and her sister Laura as they arrived at their assigned barracks. She lost no time in advising the sisters that they should look out only for themselves and no one else. *That is the only way to survive this hell,* she told them.

As time passed, my mother learned that Yuri was in fact a Czech prisoner who had been designated a *kapo* by the Nazi guards, a prisoner assigned to supervise other prisoners in exchange for such favors as extra food, cigarettes, and less-harsh treatment by the Nazis in charge. She told my mother that earlier in the war she had been one of two hundred women who had been forced to serve as sex slaves (my mother's words were less explicit) for Nazi SS soldiers. By the end of 1944, only twenty of these women remained alive. *If I lived through that, I can live through anything,* she boasted to my mother in Hungarian. However, contrary to her own advice, Yuri often secretly assisted inmates to secure food or to get easier labor assignments, sometimes taking a very young prisoner under her wing to protect her.

It was Yuri who, when the Bergen Belsen camp was liberated by the British Second Army on April 15, 1945, shouted to my mother, *Get up, Szidi. Your liberators are here! Get up! You are free!*

My mother, in a weakened state, ravaged by typhus, and having lost her only remaining sister at the camp two months earlier, could barely hear Yuri's words. Yet Yuri's strength and courage, combined with her compassion in the face of the harshest conditions, remained with my mother for the rest of her life.

She vas rough, but I loved her, my mother commented when telling me this story more than once.

It is possible that Yuri's kindhearted strength became a model for my mother's later inner resolve to move forward with her life, to raise a child totally on her own and become self-sufficient, no matter the odds. Whatever had motivated my mother's toughness, resilience, and determination, I was the lucky recipient of it after all.

CHAPTER 14

The Power of Education

My mother stressed the importance of education from the time I was five, when I already knew a college education was definitely in my future.

> *Hanele, you lucky, dey gonna put you in first grade right avay, no kindergarten. You vill go to college sooner.*
> *Why do I have to go to college, ma?*
> *Because some day you gonna be an important person in America. Dat's vhy.*
> *Do I have to go to college to be important?*
> *Yes, dat's it.*

. . . meaning there was no more room for discussion on this topic.

It was clear from the start that the *grine* wanted their children to be highly educated. Since they had bought into the American dream quickly, they knew that in order for their children to prosper in the United States, they would need to excel in school and attain the best education possible. To drive this point home to their children, they did not speak their native languages with them, only English. They might talk to one another or even hold a one-way conversation in their home language, but their offspring could respond only in English. Yiddish, however, was just too pervasive to avoid, so many of the kids understood and spoke this common tongue.

The *grine's* focus on the importance of speaking English probably accounts for the fact that, despite having grown up in a multilingual environment, I am fluent in only one language: English.

In the beginning, fearing their children would become assimilated too rapidly into a Christian America, many of the *grine* chose to enroll them in the new religious school in a stately mansion on Sumner Avenue in the Forest Park neighborhood of Springfield, the Lubavitcher Yeshiva. We would gain a solid foundation in Jewish customs, holidays, the Torah, and Hebrew, and also such secular studies as reading, arithmetic, spelling, and penmanship.

The author and her third-grade class on the grounds of the Lubavitcher Yeshiva, Sumner Avenue, 1954-55. The author is in the second row, kneeling on the far left.

Not only were the lunches delicious, cooked by one of the *grine*, Mrs. Geyser, but also the full curriculum proved to be challenging and stimulating for young students starting at the age of four. My adoration of the young principal, Rabbi David Edelman, was no secret. More than any man I had met in my early life, he was the paternal figure who made the most significant impression on me. His full beard and mustache, his dark hair, always covered by either a yarmulke or fedora, and his business suit with a peek of the *tzitzit* (fringes representing God's commandments) that hung outside his vest, made him even more appealing to me.

Sometimes in the morning, I saw the rabbi praying while wearing his *tefillin,* the phylacteries wrapped around his head and one arm, as part of the daily morning ritual that represents a Jewish male's devotion to God. Without a male figure in my household, I rarely saw this sight, so I watched our rabbi in rapture and curiosity, convinced that the ritual gave proof of the rabbi's fascinating masculinity. I certainly would not have minded being one of the numerous children the rabbi already had in his family.

On a winter day in 1955, one of the four-year-old students on the bus home from the Yeshiva was accidently killed. Shortly after disembarking, the child ran back to pick up a snowball behind the bus as it pulled away and was run over by the bus's rear wheels. At seven years old, although I did not see the accident, I was identified as a key witness and spent the next few years entangled in the legal system until someone finally realized the truth: I had not witnessed the tragic scene. True to our pattern, however, my mother and I never spoke of my connection to the accident.

The following fall, just after turning eight, I enrolled in public school and started the fourth grade at Lincoln Elementary School. My Jewish religious education, however, was not neglected upon my transfer to a public school. Most of the students at the Springfield Hebrew Institute on Chestnut Street, where I began attending several days a week after school, were the children of the enclave of Jewish survivors in Springfield's North End.

Mr. Zagorin was my Hebrew School teacher beginning in the fourth grade. By the time I had met him, he was well into his retirement years. His head held only a few white hairs in random spots, exposing his mostly bald scalp. He was markedly stooped over and hesitant in his movements. The rims of his eyes were outlined by bright red circles, making him look as though he had not slept for a month. I was not sure whether he was American born or had immigrated to Springfield from one European country or another, but he looked weathered and beaten down, as though he had been through a great ordeal earlier in his life.

Poor Mr. Zagorin could never quite remember the correct spelling of either my first or last name and consistently used an incorrect spelling on all my notices and report cards. He would miss an "n" here and place an extra "a" there, but I never told him about it. His face already looked so sad and forlorn, I did not want to bother him with the trivial matter of a slight misspelling.

Besides, he consistently had his hands full with our unruly class, whose students took advantage of his advanced age and his inability to respond quickly to their devious behavior. Using the formal manner displayed by the *grine* when addressing one another, he called us all by our surnames.

Mr. Fryman, can you read this passage in the siddur for me? Read it loud, please, so I can hear you, Mr. Zagorin asked Eddie Fryman, the boy who had recently arrived in Springfield with his mother. Even though he was several years older than I was, Eddie was placed in my Hebrew class, having a great deal of catching up to do.

Okay, but somebody just threw a spitball at the back of my head. I gotta find who it was, so can you wait a minute, Mr. Zagorin? responded Eddie, turning around in his seat,

REPORT CARD

רשימת ההתקדמות

Springfield Hebrew Institute

557 CHESTNUT ST.,   SPRINGFIELD, MASS.

Phone 9-4405

NAME *Pearlstein Hana* שם התלמיד

CLASS *4 B* המחלקה ROOM .... החדר

TEACHER *Zagorin* המורה

TERM BEGINNING .... הזמן

TO PARENTS:

The school is trying to aid the development of your child. Full growth of a Jewish child is possible only through Jewish Learning and Jewish Living. For the best results both in school and outside of school, your help is needed.

The principal and the teacher will be pleased to talk matters over with you.

1955 report card from the Springfield Hebrew Institute, signed by I. Zagorin

dispelling any notion of shyness he may have shown upon his arrival in America, and shouting, *Who threw the spitball? C'mon, just tell me who it was. I'll go easy on you.*

Mr. Fryman, turn around and face front. You need to start reading the Hebrew in your siddur! Mr. Zagorin said in the loudest voice he could muster, but it was still too feeble to arouse any discipline among his students. Eddie had already stood up from his seat and was roaming the classroom, taunting the rest of the students, and trying to finger the one who had thrown the spitball. Mr. Zagorin lost complete control of the class. Under those circumstances, it usually took him quite some time to rally his students back to their Hebrew lessons.

Despite his fragility, he had a vast knowledge of the Torah, Jewish history, and customs. I learned a lot from him based on the life lessons in the Hebrew Bible. In addition, the grades he reported for me, which included all "A"s and "B+"s, also helped to assuage any concerns I may have had over his having misspelled my name. Moreover, I always maintained my compassion for a learned man who had great knowledge to convey. If only his class would have listened.

From the fourth grade on, my mother began to monitor my grades more closely than she had before, while ensuring that I was always the best-dressed girl in my class. I began my marathon of ever-changing fashions at a very early age and have never stopped. At the same time, with my introduction to public school, I began to develop my independent nature, in part by emulating my mother, but also partly because I could write and speak English better than she could.

If I were absent from school, with her permission, I always wrote my own parental note, explaining the reasons for my absence. I also signed my mother's name. That led to many instances when I represented my mother, either verbally or in writing, with teachers, government officials, creditors, and in our mostly unsuccessful struggle to secure reparation from the German government. After considerable practice, I grew better at signing her name than she could, a potentially powerful skill, one that would have been dangerous in the wrong hands. Still, I abused the privilege only a few times later in my adolescent years for purposes that will remain unexplained.

The ability to act on my mother's behalf at a very young age offered great responsibility as well as a feeling of power and independence. I relished my growing skill at representing her and often inserted my own thoughts and opinions in written form. My talent was evident in composing such notes as the following to my much-adored sixth grade teacher, Mr. Fisk:

November 7, 1957

Dear Mr. Fisk,

Please excuse Hanna's absence on Monday and Tuesday. She had a really bad sore throat and could not swallow at all. I know she missed some of the practice examples you did in class for the spelling test, but don't worry, because she kept up with her homework and I am sure she is ready.

Sincerely,
Sidonia Perlstein

By the mid-1950s, we on Osgood Street had all made the transfer from the private religious school to a public education. Despite their struggles with the English language, the *grine* focused on their children's school progress with laser-like precision. Although the academic abilities of their children varied, some eventually becoming National Merit Scholars while some barely attaining passing grades, the expectations did not differ much. They were all expected to go on to higher education and enter an honorable and, hopefully, lucrative profession.

I remember how the whole community watched as one of the older children who had completed college applied to medical school. Not only did the applicant and his parents wait for the responses to his applications, but the entire universe of *grine* also waited with them. His journey to medical school was probably much more public than it would have been in any other community. In a sense, he was a test case, allowing everyone to evaluate how their own children might be treated as they followed in his footsteps.

When rejection letter followed rejection letter, everyone was buzzing about the possible reasons and what would happen to Barry, the student in the fish bowl.

Vhat could be da reason vhy dey are turning him avay? questioned Mr. Feinberg. *He is such a good student.*

Ya, he deserve to be a doctor, said his wife.

Maybe dey not taking any more Jewish students dis year, Mr. Feinberg added.

The rejections might have been a vestige of the Jewish quotas that plagued entrance to colleges and graduate schools until the mid-twentieth century. No one knew for sure. The community was disappointed, but in the end, Barry went to pharmacy school and became a successful pharmacist, well known and respected in the Springfield area. His resilience and motivation to succeed despite his earlier rejections set an example for the rest of the children as they grew and faced similar challenges.

CHAPTER 15

Restitution of a Life

1955. My mother and I began a strange, circuitous, and highly discouraging odyssey when I was eight years old. We attempted to obtain a semblance of restitution for the crimes my mother had endured during and because of the Holocaust. Entering a world of legal bureaucracy that would confuse, befuddle, and humiliate any human being who dared to enter its labyrinth, we nevertheless vowed to continue the journey — ultimately, a forty-year, tiresome expedition — until we reached its final conclusion. I should clarify that my mother traversed the journey toward restitution mostly on her own, since I was either too young or too disinterested until much later to join her.

Wiedergutmachung, the German word for reparation, or restitution, was a misnomer. Breaking the word into its parts, *wieder-gut-machung* means 'to make good again,' to restore life's condition to its status before the incident that destroyed it. The *grine* knew full well that nothing could restore their lives to their former state. No reparations could bring about a change to the loss of family, homes, health, and livelihoods. They would have to live without those lost treasures for the rest of their lives. Yet, when the German government announced they had agreed to pay *Wiedergutmachung* to Holocaust victims, all the *grine* decided to pursue the possibility. In truth, to most of them, it was much more a matter of restored morality than financial gain.

In 1955, a decade after the close of World War II and the liberation of Holocaust survivors, my mother opened her restitution case, along with the rest of Springfield's survivors and thousands of others around the world. The West German Parliament had recently passed legislation known as the *Bundesentschädigungsgesetz,* the Federal Indemnification Law, to compensate the victims of National Socialist persecution. The key for the applicant was to satisfy the law by providing indisputable proof of loss of life, damage to limb or health, loss of liberty, property, possessions, or vocational or economic pursuits — an exceedingly more difficult task than it would seem on the surface.

I had no knowledge of the particulars of anyone else's compensation case except my mother's, although I understood that every family in my community dealt with the bureaucracies of a reticent German restitution system. As a child, I could never fully understand its various elements. However, I looked forward to our train trips to New York City, where my mother was summoned on many occasions to visit the New York offices of the United Restitution Organization, commonly known as the URO. The URO was charged with providing legal assistance to the claimants under the auspices of the Conference on Jewish Material Claims, or Claims Conference. It was on those trips that we also visited our distant American relatives in the Bronx, who always welcomed us with open arms and with conversation in both Hungarian and English. For my mother, the tension of pursuing her compensation case was buffered by the unconditional warmth and affection she received from these cousins.

As a child, I identified the URO only as the transmitter of negative news. After receiving each one of hundreds of documents over the years from that agency, my mother lay on the couch in our living room and just stared at the ceiling, closing herself off from the world, and from me.

On a visit to our New York cousins, early 1950s

For some reason, perhaps to remind myself of my mother's arduous journey to gain recompense for her painful life, her loss of liberty, her physical and mental impairments, and everything she held dear, I have kept at least some of the files containing the reparation case correspondence in both English and German submitted by the URO. The documents pertain mainly to her mental and physical injuries — her lifelong depression and anxiety, her incessant insomnia, and her constant leg pain from severe varicose veins and an untreated leg fracture incurred at Dachau. She further suffered from intestinal discomfort and pain, and finally, the loss of most of, and eventually, all her teeth. Could she prove that those ailments stemmed from or were aggravated by her time as a slave laborer in three concentration camps? Had they impeded her ability to work after her experience was over? I offer a brief account of her continued journey in this volume since it sheds rare insight into one survivor's struggle for justice.

The first letter brought news about an award of compensation for my mother's loss of liberty during her period of internment:

United Restitution Organization (URO) — New York Office
December 2, 1958

Dear Mrs. Perlstein:
We are glad to be able to inform you that the Indemnification Office in Hannover has granted you for damage to your liberty during 12 months the amount of DM 1.800.

It will be remitted to you by dollar check within two to three months directly from Germany. Our office in Germany will deduct the fee agreed upon.

We still have to work on the damage to your health. We, therefore, ask you to come to our office for an interview with Dr. Walter Hein . . . .

Sincerely yours,
Dr. Walter Hein

The equivalent of DM (Deutsche Marks) 1.800 in American dollars was about $430. My mother did not seem to complain about the insignificant amount of recompense for her loss of liberty. But I always wondered how anyone could place a monetary value on such a thing as the loss of liberty. "Liberty" means 'the quality or state of being free: the power to do as one pleases, freedom from physical restraint, freedom from arbitrary or despotic control, the positive enjoyment of various social, political or economic rights and privileges, the power of choice' *(Merriam-Webster Dictionary).* Since my mother had lost those freedoms, in truth, for many years before her actual deportation, and since she had left to build a new

United Restitution Organization (URO)
NEW YORK OFFICE
1241 BROADWAY • NEW YORK 1, N. Y. • Phone MUrray Hill 5-5900 • Cable Address Amfedera, New York

December 2, 1958

Mrs. Sidonia Perlstein
64 Osgood Street
Springfield, Mass.

Our Ref.:
C-WE-lk
To be quoted in your reply.
(Angabe dieses Aktenzeichens dringend erbeten.)

Dear Mrs. Perlstein:

We are glad to be able to inform you that the Indemnification
Office in HANNOVER has granted you for damage to your liberty
during 12 months the amount of

DM 1.800.-.

It will be remitted to you by dollarcheck within two to three
months directly from Germany. Our office in Germany will deduct the fee agreed upon.

We still will have to work on the damage to your health. We,
therefore, ask you to come to our office for an interview with
Dr. Walter Hein on
Tuesday, January 6, 1959 at 2 o'clock p.m.

Sincerely yours,

A letter from the United Restitution Organization

life in the shadow of her losses, how could $430 be considered proper compensation? I found it absurd.

To my mother, the more significant loss, even more than her loss of liberty, was the murder of every member of her nuclear family and most of her extended relatives. Nothing could replace that overwhelming blow — four hundred or four million. It did not seem to matter. No further correspondence appears in the files with regard to any complaint about this settlement.

Believing that she could not show proof of property losses, she focused her attention on the permanent damage to her health, and particularly her mental health. Surely, the German Federal Indemnification Court would realize the heavy toll her internment had taken on her body and soul. Indeed, it took every bit of time and stamina she could muster to pursue this aspect of her claim.

The first hint of how the German Indemnification Office

would treat her case arrived two years later, expressed in the following letter:

January 11, 1961

Dear Mrs. Perlstein:

The indemnification office in Hannover suggested an agreement the terms of which are contained in the enclosed copy. . . . We informed you that the doctors recognized you to have been disabled more than 25% only until December 31, 1956. From January 1, 1957 on, your disability amounted merely to 20%.

Therefore, the German indemnification authority offers to pay you:

For the time of liberation until January 1, 1953: . . .

Then, for the time from November 1, 1953 until December 31, 1955 . . .

Consequently you would be paid the sum of . . . DM 10.300 or $2,580.

Besides, you can claim the expenses you had for medical treatment of

> *Gall bladder trouble*
>
> *Nervousness and depression*
>
> *Treatment of your teeth . . . apart from the payment mentioned above.*

Please inform us whether you agree with this settlement. . . . We wish to add that in case you do not want to accept the settlement, the indemnification office is probably going to issue a decision in no way different. . . . You would have to file a complaint in the course of which you must prove that you have been disabled more than 25% beyond December 31, 1956.

As we stated before, the medical certificate . . . confirms what the German doctors alleged, namely that after the gall

*bladder operation you were quite well and the broken leg
healed without noticeable consequences. . . .*

*Sincerely yours,
Dr. Walter Hein*

As I perused the voluminous pile of documents relating to this case,
I assumed my mother was not willing to accept the decision of the
indemnification authority. Throughout the 1960s and up until the
1990s, appeal followed appeal, and rejection followed rejection.
Could my mother's delicate mental health withstand the ordeal of
seeking justice?

Another three years passed, bringing the case into 1964, when
the following letter arrived:

March 23, 1964

*Dear Mrs. Perlstein,
We are attaching a copy of the additional opinion rendered
by experts of the Annastift Clinic in Hannover-Kleefeld. As
you will note, the opinion is unfavorable. . . . You will be kept
informed...*

*Sincerely yours,
Dr. [the German title for an attorney] N. Klinefeld*

This discouraging news was followed only three days later by what
I have always viewed as a highly offensive, uninformed, and humiliating letter:

*March 26, 1964
IMPAIRMENT OF HEALTH*

Dear Mrs. Perlstein,

...The main consideration in the opinion of the Annastift Clinic is ... that you had an occupation, which required constant standing already in the years prior to the persecution; and that ... has brought about ... the varicosity of your veins.

We suggest that you name witnesses, or indicate other evidentiary material, to show that no varicosity was apparent prior to the persecution or at the beginning of your confinement in Auschwitz. Of course, only such persons might come into consideration who had an opportunity to see you in some bathing establishment or swimming places.

You should also inform us in full detail, [including the] name[s] [of] witnesses, about the extent of your work in a standing position; we assume that you did not have to be on your feet all the time.

Sincerely yours,
Dr. N. Klinefeld

Although I am unsure of my mother's reaction to this letter, it struck me that the attorney who wrote it did not know much about his client. Engulfed by thousands of applications for restitution, it was probably impossible for him and his colleagues to know each applicant's background. Only someone who was totally unaware of my mother's upbringing could have made the requests found in the letter.

Raised as a strictly Orthodox Jew in a little hamlet in Hungary, where Jewish women religiously covered most of their skin, my mother would never have entered a "bathing establishment" or "swimming places." Nor did her work as a seamstress and tradesperson in Hungary require constant standing. While it was true that she possessed mild varicose veins before the war, the varicosity became exceedingly thicker, more pronounced, and more painful after her wartime experiences.

As a prisoner in three death camps, it was that span of time that took an immense toll on my mother's mind, body, and soul. Remaining on her feet with no food or water for several days in a cattle car; standing at attention for countless hours for early morning roll calls; lifting steel off trains as a slave laborer assisting the German production of fighter planes; enduring an untreated broken leg; cleaning latrines; running to work assignments and dashing naked for numerous "selections" before Nazi doctors, had undoubtedly worsened my mother's varicose veins and brought constant leg pain.

Although she had contacted one of her few surviving cousins to ask for an affidavit verifying that they had grown up together in the same village, she also knew the cousin could not attest to the required conditions. The case lingered until the next year, 1965, a decade after the first filing, when the following pivotal letters, one attached to the other, arrived from yet another attorney.

First, the legal findings, written in German, sent by the URO Hannover office to the New York office, which transmitted it to my mother:

May 20, 1965:

The aforementioned case was argued before the higher regional court in Celle on May 19, 1965. We had the opportunity to present our case in detail. . . . We suggested that the court present a settlement proposal to the parties. The counterpart declined [the right to] any further statement.

On June 2, 1965, the court will render its decision. We expect the following: The court will render a settlement proposal, according to which the petitioner should again receive a pension for a loss in earning capacity of 25% from July 1, 1963. For the time between January 1, 1957, and July 1, 1963, the petitioner should renounce any pension back payments.

After our summation, the presiding judge declared that, according to the court's experience, the evaluation of the gallbladder ailment at 20% after an operation is excessive. It is remarkable that the bouts of depression, although noted, should generate absolutely no measurable loss of earning capacity. Should the court have to consider an expert opinion regarding the varicose veins, it can be certainly predicted that such an additional expert opinion would be to the detriment of the petitioner, as in fact, in the numerous cases that the panel [of judges] has had to decide upon, not a single case has been known where varicose veins have been recognized as having been caused by the persecution. The prevailing German view is that this [illness] is always due to a congenital weakness of the connective tissue.

In the present case, particularly the splayfeet exhibited by the petitioner and the fact that the left leg as well as the damaged right leg shows varicose veins support this. On the other hand, the panel would like to follow our suggestion of a settlement proposal because the report by the Annastift Clinic is actually somewhat contradictory. It is really not clear why a job requiring standing for long periods ("predisposing factor") should promote varicose veins, but standing for roll call in a concentration camp should not.

We ask even now to discuss with the petitioner whether we are allowed to accept such a court-mandated settlement proposal, which we confidently expect, as we will certainly receive only a very short deadline for our reply. Regardless of this, upon receipt of the settlement proposal, we will naturally immediately transmit it to you.

P.S. The compensation panel will propose the course of the pension only from the year 1963 because, in the expected final law, the presumption [of damage] in the case of a concentration camp stay of longer than one year will also lead only to compensation from 1963.

The above letter was attached to the official notice of settlement, written in English, dated two weeks later:

June 4, 1965

Dear Mrs. Perlstein,
   . . . According to this letter, the court is making a proposition of settlement according to which you would receive starting with July 1963 a monthly pension of at least DM 147. This amount is based on a reduction of your working ability of 25%.
   Will you please inform me as soon as possible whether you would be willing to close a settlement on this basis?

Sincerely yours,
Dr. R. Mendelsohn

Finally, an offer was presented for a monthly pension to compensate for my mother's physical suffering. When read more carefully, however, combined with a review of the actual hearing results from Hannover, the offer may have sounded less and less generous to my mother. The amount offered of 147 deutsche marks equivalent to about $37 a month, or $444 a year, in 1965 (depending on the exchange rate), was exceedingly low, even by 1965 standards. At the time, my mother never imagined she would live until 2006. Even then, over the next forty years of her life, the cumulative amount would have been relatively insubstantial.

   Yet, if she had been able to read and sufficiently comprehend the court's ruling in German, she may have gleaned that this was, most likely, the court's final offer to compensate for her health damages in the form of a pension. It may have been her inadequate knowledge of the language, her frustration at the lack of recognition of her mental suffering, or her determination to receive the full compensation she felt her case warranted that led her to refuse the settlement and submit another appeal of the ruling. In doing so, she had unwittingly closed the window of opportunity for any future meaningful consideration of her case. However, as a budding adolescent, I put any further thoughts about my mother's compensation case aside for the time being.

CHAPTER 16

A Community Still Vulnerable

The horrible school bus accident in which little Benny had lost his life was a shock to everyone in our community. The tragedy would have had an impact on any neighborhood, but it hit the *grine* even harder. They had all survived seemingly insurmountable odds to immigrate to a new country and reinvent their lives with their young children. It was inconceivable that such an event could erase the life of such a little, innocent boy born in their adopted land.

The boy's mother and father and older brother, Melvin, were numb for a while, unable to absorb the reality of Benny's death. I visited them in their Osgood Street apartment a few times after the accident, feeling some of their pain and grief since I had been identified as the key witness to the awful episode. Their sad and mournful faces haunted me for some time.

> *I wish I could have done something so the accident didn't happen*, I said to Benny's mother.
> *No, Hanele, ve understand. Dere is noting you could do. Oy, he vas such a malekh* [an angel], Mrs. Kazinsky replied, reassuring me.

For weeks, the atmosphere around the *grine* was filled with sorrow and silence as everyone processed the shock of this event. Even my friends among the community were so dumbstruck by the accident and so absorbed in the ensuing sadness, that some of them, who were nowhere near the events of that day, felt as though they had personally participated in the horrible incident. The bus accident was vividly recalled and described by everyone — children and adults — whether present at the scene or not.

Nevertheless, in a spirit of resilience, only a year after the dreadful loss of their youngest son, Mr. and Mrs. Kazinsky produced a new child, their daughter, Lisa. It did not take very long for them to discover that Lisa had been born with congenital disabilities that left her unable to speak, walk, or move most of her body and confined her to a wheelchair. Her arms and legs erupted in frequent spasms. The family seemed to take Lisa's disability in stride, showering her with their affection and attention. I used to see them outside taking walks together as a family on Dwight Street, Mr. Kazinsky pushing Lisa's wheelchair and bending over to kiss her on the cheek. But after their daughter's birth, Mr. and Mrs. Kazinsky's melancholy faces seemed permanent.

Within the next few years, two adult losses reminded the community they were still vulnerable to the same diseases and infirmities as the population as a whole. Though they had lost so much already in their lives, they were not immune to more such bereavement in their near future.

One morning, I heard the strange, unfamiliar sound of ambulance sirens coming toward our apartment block. As I gazed out my mother's bedroom window, the one that faced the street, I saw the emergency medical technicians carry a stretcher through the doorway leading to the other side of our building. A few minutes later, they returned to go out the same door.

I tried to make out the face of the man lying supine on the stretcher. I could tell it was a tall form, exceptional for our community, which led me to think it was Mr. Rath, a long-legged, lean, spectacled man, known for his quiet, unassuming nature. As they moved him into the rear of the ambulance, I realized it was Mr. Lott, his eyes closed and his face ashen. I yelled for my mother.

Ma, ma, it's Mr. Lott. The ambulance is taking him away. Do you know what is happening?

My mother came to the window and expressed her surprise. *No, no, I don't know. I going to his apartment to see if I can find his vayb* [wife].

Okay, can I come with you?

Yeh, let's go an see vhat happen an if ve can help, my mother said resolutely.

We went to the Lott's apartment and found only his thirteen-year-old son, Leo, sitting on a kitchen chair, while other tenants from our apartment building entered at the same time. His mother had jumped into the back of the ambulance with her husband to accompany him to the hospital, leaving Leo on his own.

It was his heart, Leo said to us with a solemn face. *It just gave out. I think he is gone.* Everyone waited in the apartment with Leo for the next hour, when Mrs. Lott called to say that her husband had died. A sudden heart attack had killed him at the age of forty-five. He had been a lab technician at the same dental laboratory as Mr. Goodman, manufacturing dentures. Now his wife would have to be the sole breadwinner.

Lena Lott was one of my mother's best friends among the *grine*. A short, round-faced woman with jet-black hair, she worked as a clerk at Ruby's Market on nearby Dwight Street. She had taken time to get to know my mother, and therefore, may have known some of her secrets. She and Mr. Lott's sister, Mania, were close enough to my mother to call her by her first name. They were among the few who had that privilege. I noticed that most of our immigrant group had polite interactions with my mother, but they must have gleaned from her outer veneer that she would not allow them to get close enough to ask any personal questions about her past. Lena and Mania were true exceptions.

Invitations had already gone out for Leo Lott's bar mitzvah, which was scheduled for the following week, but due to his father's death, the event was cancelled. Leo's bar mitzvah was postponed and ended up as a low-key service in the synagogue with no reception.

Mr. Lott had lived through the Holocaust with his wife and sister and baby Leo underground in a hole dug under a farmer's barn. They were hidden by the Christian farmer and his family at the risk of their own deaths at the hands of Nazi soldiers. The farmer's family had provided food for the Lotts, removed their waste, and took care of other living necessities, all the while keeping the life-and-death secret of harboring Jews on their property. Mr. Lott had lived in fear of being discovered for at least two years in a dark, airless earthen bunker, stifling his little baby's cries lest they be heard and give away their location. He had survived those extremely adverse conditions during the war, but after living a dozen or so more years, his heart could stand no more.

Just a couple of months later, Mr. Geyser, the husband of the talented Yeshiva cook, also suffered a massive heart attack that quickly stole his life, despite being only in his forties, like Mr. Lott. He was noted for his magnificent singing voice, entertaining the *grine* on many occasions with his impromptu familiar Yiddish songs. His wife was a close relative, and perhaps their shared memories of life in Poland sparked their love after the war, leading to their marriage.

Mr. Geyser and his wife had traveled to Sweden soon after their liberation to live with his brother. However, their ultimate goal was to realize the dream of going to America, so they waited in Sweden until they could obtain the proper visas to enter the United States. Arriving in Springfield with their little daughter, Sandra, around the same time as the rest of the *grine,* in 1949, they did not live in our block. They rented a second-floor apartment in a two-story house at the other end of Osgood Street, near the corner of Main Street, where Mr. Geyser's wife and daughter remained after his death.

I have always found it strange that I have recollected the faces of little Benny and of these men who died a few short years after their arrival even more than many other faces among my immigrant group. Their early demise must have planted a permanent marker in my brain, one that has instinctively caused them to stand out in my mind. I guess to me, the men's deaths were akin to that of the American soldier who had been a prisoner of war in Vietnam for many years only to lose his life in a car accident shortly after being released. Each had used all their will to survive, and then fate arranged a short aftermath.

Part Two: Acculturation

CHAPTER 17

The Girl of Summer

I never had a happier day in my life up to that point than October 4, 1955. That was the day the Brooklyn Dodgers finally won the World Series. By that time, I was an old hat at watching the veteran Brooklyn team, having seen them on television over the spring and summer. I knew all the players' names and their positions on the team and could recognize their faces as though they were my friends.

My baseball mentor was Mrs. Harris, who took care of me in the afternoons soon after I started public school. Mrs. Harris and her husband and daughter also lived on the third floor in our Osgood Street building at the other end of our back porch. I had only to go out of my back door from our kitchen and walk a short stretch down the porch to arrive at the Harris's back door. Mr. Harris worked several jobs, including selling newspapers and magazines at a newsstand downtown, which limited the time he could spend with his family. I rarely saw him. The Harrises were not members of the *grine*, just a Jewish family that worked hard but could not afford a more expensive place to live, like everyone else in our building.

Mrs. Harris had been born and bred in Brooklyn, New York. A hefty, down-to-earth woman, she had stringy dark-brown hair and glasses and usually wore a plain housedress. She did not seem to care much about her looks, focusing more on making sure the bills were paid and fanatically rooting for her favorite team. You could tell immediately by her accent and team allegiance she was not from Springfield, Massachusetts.

Dem bums. Dose Dodgers are tryin' my patience. When in heck do ya think they'll come around and win the series, huh? I can't take it no more.

Yeah, you're right, I said. *When are they finally gonna win?*

Pushing her stringy hair aside, she said, *I'm countin' on Duke and Campanella this year. I'm hopin' they'll finally come through.*

Let's keep our fingers crossed, I replied, holding up the crossed fingers of both my hands.

Most of our conversations that year revolved around the Dodgers and the phenomenal season they were having. For me to share Mrs. Harris's zeal about "dem bums," I had to know the rules of the game, the plays, the stats, and the players. Many of the games were played in mid-afternoon, so I could catch only the last portion of them after school. But when they played on weekends, I usually went over to Mrs. Harris's apartment to watch the game with her.

My mother seemed amused by my immersion in baseball, although it was a game totally foreign to her. She had played ball as a child in her home village, but from her description, it seemed more like soccer than baseball or American football. In her desire to ensure my Americanization as intensely as possible, she was supportive and even encouraging of my baseball friendship with Mrs. Harris.

Sure, Hanele, if it's okay mit Mrs. Harris, you can go over to vatch da games. I tink it's a good idea.

Thanks, ma. If you're interested, I'll let you know how the Dodgers are doing, I said, even though I knew she would have little interest in my reports.

*Tank you. Dat vould be nice. Just a qvestion, Hanele. Is
dere a team fun [from] Massachusett?* she asked, as usual
leaving off the final 's' in "Massachusetts."

*Yeah, ma. There's the Red Sox, but my team is the Dodgers.
I just love them. I could never root for a different team.*

My head that summer was filled with runs batted in, sacrifice flies,
homers, batting averages, and wins and losses. Names like Pee
Wee Reese, Jackie Robinson, Duke Snider, Gil Hodges, and Roy
Campanella slipped off my tongue as easily as those of my school-
mates. I was heady with the prospect of my team possibly winning
the pennant and going to the World Series again for the eighth time.
They had not won any of the seven times they had achieved the
National League's championship and played for the trophy in the
past, but I was sure this would be their year.

It would not be exaggerating to say that when the Dodgers
did win the pennant, Mrs. Harris became my best friend. I was
an eight-year-old girl with a Brooklyn-born homemaker as my
closest buddy. The Dodgers would again play the venerable New
York Yankees for the World Series title. Then, from September 28 to
October 4, 1955, Mrs. Harris and I were almost inseparable. Even
though her husband and daughter were also fans, they did not seem
to have the same kind of enthusiasm as I had. My indoctrination
into the world of the Dodgers was complete.

The first two games of the series were played at Yankee Stadium
on a Wednesday and Thursday. When I came home from school on
the first day, Mrs. Harris was standing up in front of her television
set screaming at her team. The game was already at the bottom of
the eighth.

*Hi, Hanna. We're down by only one, only one stupid run.
Duke and Carl Furillo both homered, and Jackie Robinson*

Views of 64-68 Osgood Street

stole home in the first inning. There's still a chance that they
could score in the ninth.

But the Dodgers did not score in the ninth and lost the first game
six to five. They lost the second game as well and the mood was
bleak. When my mother came home from work, she could not help
but notice that I was terribly distressed. My team had lost the first
two games of the series. Things were looking grim, and I must have
worn my gloom on my face.

> *Vhat's wrong mit you, Hanele?* she asked.
> *Oh, nothing. Just baseball,* I responded.

I could see her mouth curl up into a little grin. She was genuinely
enjoying my deep involvement with American baseball.

The third game was played across town in Brooklyn, at Ebbets
Field. When I arrived that day, Mrs. Harris had a wide smile on her
face. She already knew by the eighth inning that the Dodgers were
going to win. I watched the last inning with her, and we screamed
together when the Dodgers won eight to three. Roy Campanella
had homered and Johnny Podres, who was not one of the players I
knew very well, was the lucky pitcher.

Over that weekend, I pretty much lived at the Harris's apartment. My mother reminded me we had a new television set, a Philco
console, which had arrived in June, and I could watch the games at
home if I wanted. She usually spent weekends lying down on the
living room couch, her legs lifted up on a pillow, often nursing a
severe headache and trying to de-stress from her demanding work-
week. On most Saturday mornings, after our television arrived, I
watched my favorite show, *Winky Dink and You.* Once I received
my *Winky Dink* kit in the mail, I used that sheet of plastic to cover
the TV screen, and with the accompanying crayons, I could decode

any message Winky was sending to all the kids watching at home. No other kid was more faithful to Winky than I was.

But I could not watch a baseball game without the company of Mrs. Harris, so I left my mother on her sofa and ran down the back porch to enter the world of baseball. Part of the fun was joining Mrs. Harris for our own rooting section more than a hundred miles away from New York.

The Dodgers played at Ebbets Field again, and to our riotous response, won both of the weekend games. Roy and Duke and Gil had again come through. Our team was ahead in the series by three games to two. I held hands with Mrs. Harris, praying they would win it all the next day.

On Monday, the rollercoaster of our emotions went down again. By the time I arrived at Mrs. Harris's apartment that day, it was the ninth inning and the Dodgers were losing five to one. No score in the ninth meant the game was lost and the series was tied. The next day, Tuesday, October 4, would decide whether all my investment of time and devotion to a team I knew only because my neighbor had instilled a love of the game in me would ultimately result in supreme joy or bitter disappointment.

The last game was as tense as it gets. I had spent the day at my new school, Lincoln Elementary, but unbeknown to everyone, including my teacher, I was thinking about the Dodgers every moment. When I arrived home, I went straight to Mrs. Harris's apartment and saw her sitting at the edge of her recliner bracing herself. Again, the game was at the eighth inning and the Yankees were scoreless. The Dodgers were up two to nothing.

No homers yet. Gil Hodges hit a single and a sacrifice fly early on. That's how they scored. It looks like they might do it. They just might do it, she squealed.

Gee, I'm glad I got home just in time to maybe see them win it all, I said in excitement.

In the end, pitcher Johnny Podres had kept the Yankees from scoring. The game was over. The Dodgers had won the World Series. Sheer pandemonium erupted at Yankee Stadium among the Dodgers fans and also in the Harris's little living room. Oh, the supreme joy!

The Dodgers won the pennant again in 1956 and played the Yankees again in the World Series. Mrs. Harris and I had followed them all season, and we experienced many of the same emotions of the previous year. The bums had brought us to the brink again, taking the series all the way to the seventh game but had lost in a shutout to the Yankees.

By 1958, the Dodgers had left Brooklyn and moved to Los Angeles, leaving a throng of ardent Brooklyn fans to lament their loss. I was not from Brooklyn, just a fanatic Massachusetts schoolgirl enamored of a fabled New York team and with a newfound outlet for pent-up emotion. But the Dodgers were no longer the same team to me either. Although I was disappointed at their move, my time with the Dodgers taught me some valuable lessons.

First, no other activity could have made me feel more American than my fanatical immersion into baseball. My involvement was accidental, having as my neighbor a devoted fan and caretaker. However, once Mrs. Harris introduced me to the game, I was mesmerized as I watched the players move with an almost ballet-like quality, catching a line drive and throwing the ball to the first baseman for an out, or leaping to grasp the ball as it zoomed over the field, thwarting a potential homerun. Transfixed, I admired the rapid movement of the ball as the second baseman threw to the first baseman for a double play, or the sharp clicking sound as the batter hit a fastball. Nothing else could match the exhilaration of seeing a player hit the ground to slide in for a stolen base or reach home plate. As I became a genuine baseball fan, I concurrently became the most patriotic American.

Second, I learned to have a little faith. If the Dodgers could wait to win the World Series after seven failed attempts, I could muster enough patience to achieve my goals.

Finally, as my mother intimated, I learned that when you live in Massachusett [sic], you should be rooting for the Red Sox.

CHAPTER 18

Clair de Lune

Piano was the instrument I always wanted to play. I liked to go down to the second floor to watch Sally as she practiced her piano pieces. She was far from an impresario, but nevertheless, she could play some basic piano tunes with proper seriousness and aplomb. Confident that I could learn to play at least as well, I begged my mother to buy a piano so I could begin my lessons, but she quickly squashed my plan.

Ma, now that I'm eight, I think I'm ready to start taking piano lessons. Could we buy a piano soon? I asked.

Oy, Hanele. I vish I could buy a piano for you. It vould make me very happy, but no, ve can't buy a piano right now. Ve have to save our money.

Why? Can't we take some of the money we would have saved and buy the piano?

No, it don't vork like dat. Ve don't have too much money, so ve have to save to buy da tings ve really need, like food and rent, and someday a car, and don't forget your college. You vill have to play someting else.

Lincoln Elementary School had some ideas regarding the instrument at which I could possibly excel: the violin. The music teacher, Mr. Fournier, advised me that if I could find a violin to practice with, he would make time to provide me with some extra lessons in addition to the regular school music class. Since my mother was not eager to invest in an instrument, all I had to do was find a violin — as though there were plenty in the offing.

The violinist in sixth grade at Lincoln School, 1957–58

As I had little expectation that a violin would miraculously present itself to me, I went on the offensive in my search to find one. After my mother and I spread the word of my desperate need for a violin to every member of the *grine*, the miracle occurred. Mrs. Feinberg possessed one she had brought with her from Poland, and she gladly offered it to me to use for my lessons. I did not ask until much later whether it was a gift or a loan, an omission that would ultimately lead to the most miserable consequences.

Mr. Fournier tried his best to teach me the finer techniques involved in playing the violin, one of the hardest instruments to learn, but his efforts proved to be fruitless. I never caught on to the instrument that substituted for the one I truly desired. My tone was not very elegant, sometimes sounding similar to the scratches of chalk along a blackboard. At other times, the sweet, mellow sound emanating from the curved wooden box as the horsehair bow swept across its strings fascinated me. The music somehow appealed to an inner passion I had never embraced before. With enough practice and all the patience I could muster, I could eke out the tune to my favorite violin piece, one Claude Debussy had originally composed for the piano, "Clair de Lune" (Moonlight). And I did not sound too bad.

The quietness and serenity of Clair de Lune's every note seemed to resonate with my own sense of solitude and melancholy. More than any other influence in my childhood, playing this tune on the violin captured the feelings I could not express to anyone. My mixed emotions toward my mother and feelings of loneliness and isolation had found an extraordinary channel through my violin and "Clair de Lune," even though my natural talent was negligible. Practicing that piece gave me unusual solace and comfort.

The beauty of the violin's sound kept me playing from the fourth to the eighth grade, carrying my instrument from Lincoln School all the way to Forest Park Junior High after our move. But when I was placed in the third violin section, the Siberia of the school orchestra, a place where violinists are never heard from again, I finally decided to forego my virtuoso's life and cease my practice. My frustration resulted in a tempestuous fit one night in my bedroom when I smashed the instrument to the wall and broke its graceful neck.

Hanele, vhat's going on here? Vhat is dat noise? Oy, gotenu [dear God], *you broke da violin?* my mother asked in a panic as she entered my room.

I didn't mean to do it. It's just that I finally realized I'm no good at it and I'll never be better. I didn't think it would break, I cried.

Oy, ve have tsores [troubles] *now,* she lamented. *How can I tell Mrs. Feinberg dat ve broke her violin?*

It's my fault. Anyway, she gave us the violin, right?

No, Hanele. She just loan it to us for as long as you need it. Ve had to give it back.

I was ashamed at my outburst resulting in the demolition of the violin. Although I felt inadequate as a player, I would also miss the mournful, vibrating sounds that had struck a chord in my soul. Having rarely destroyed anything in the past, however, I had unintentionally chosen the absolutely wrong thing to break.

My mother spared me the humiliation of telling Mrs. Feinberg the news about her violin and took on the task herself. Since I was not present, I am not sure what words either party spoke, but I was grateful for my mother's bravery in taking the blame in the situation. Unfortunately, I am certain we lost Mrs. Feinberg's friendship for at least the next twenty-five years. My mother and she rarely spoke to each other again until the later years of their lives, when the violin incident had disappeared from their memories.

When my mother returned from the showdown with Mrs. Feinberg that day, all she said to me was, in a deep voice, *Hanele, promise me you vill never do someting like dis again. Never. Okay?*

CHAPTER 19

The Matchmaker: Progress Report 1

My mother and I were invited to many more children's birthday parties after our initial invitation to Sally's fifth-birthday celebration. It seemed as though every weekend was busy with one party or another.

At Harry Sklarz's fourth-birthday celebration, I noticed Mr. Goodman beside a woman with short, dark hair and glasses at the party. As time went on, I had stopped trying to say hello or making small talk with him as he would never respond, always pretending that I was not in the room or looking in the other direction. I had no clue who this woman might be, but she was definitely not one of the *grine*. It seemed she was his date.

> *Ma, do you know who that lady is with Mr. Goodman?*
> *Vhat lady, Hanele?* my mother asked distractedly. *I not looking right now.*
> *I was just wondering because I don't recognize her.*
> *Me neider. I don't really care.*

It seemed that neither Mr. Goodman nor my mother cared much for each other. Their mutual disdain was quite visible. Yet he seemed very cheerful and amiable on that occasion. Uncharacteristic of his normal arrogant veneer, he showed the woman to her chair at one of the tables and made loud, lively conversation with her. When I heard her voice, I realized she was a native-born American, without the obvious accent of every member of the *grine*. He was courting an *Americanishe* (born in America or Americanized) woman.

I saw them together a few times after that and met the woman's daughter from a previous marriage. She was about my age and seemed eager to make friends with the other children among the *grine*. Soon after, Mr. Goodman married the American woman, and they bought a home together not too far away.

Mr. Goodman's marriage took him off my list of potential fathers, although for all intents and purposes, he had never really been on it, given the palpable animosity between him and my mother. Something must have happened between them, but for a long time I never knew what it was or asked about it.

Even though he had never been a real contender, Mr. Goodman's marrying increased my pressure to get closer to the other *grine* bachelors before all of them were taken by other women and, therefore, unavailable to my mother.

CHAPTER 20

The Somnambulist

Many children had only a sketchy knowledge of their parents' past, their horrific experiences and losses, the particulars of their former lives, and their difficulties in adjusting to a new universe. At the same time, the children were fearful of asking too many questions, always trying to keep a delicate balance between their parents' and their own emotional equilibrium.

My circumstances were a little different than that of my peers. My mother took every opportunity, especially at mealtimes, to tell me in vivid detail about her childhood, her siblings, and her terrible experiences during the Holocaust. But she could never impart what I really wanted to hear. What happened to my father? I could muster the nerve to ask only once, when I was six years old. Her cold nonreply set the pattern for the rest of our life together. That was the line I could never cross.

Like many children of refugees who may repeatedly hear tales of suffering, I needed to develop my own coping mechanisms. For example, I used to be a somnambulist. As far as I know, I exhibited that bizarre behavior only for a two-week period when I was nine and have not suffered from it since. Aside from remembering the bedroom in which it began, I have no recollection of any of my purported actions during my brief encounter with sleepwalking. The episode coincidentally happened after my mother's sudden gallstone attack.

Since I lived with the only person who was my whole family, I also lived in perpetual fear that something would happen to remove her from my life, and consequently, leave me on my own. I was prone to following my mother around very closely in my early childhood, even accompanying her like a puppy on her brief trips down to the end of the back porch to dispose of our weekly trash in the incinerator chute.

Public school and Hebrew school kept me occupied most weekdays. Mrs. Harris kept me busy after school, especially during baseball season. At other times, I looked forward to my mother coming home from work to confirm she was still around and would continue to care for me. Even though I often had mixed emotions about her, the thought of losing her made me shudder.

One day, in the winter of 1956, we were sitting at our kitchen table after just having finished our supper. I was looking out the window, the one located on the wall adjacent to the table, ready to begin one of my regular daydreams, when my mother started to entertain me with a story about growing up in her childhood village, Dámóc. Looking away from the window and down at the gray Formica tabletop, I was not sure whether I wanted to hear another one of her stories, which would interrupt my anticipated daydream. This particular tale was about her athletic prowess as a youth playing sports with her siblings and the other children in her village. As she stopped to pause in her storytelling, she began to grimace in pain. Grabbing her upper belly, she seemed to be having great difficulty catching her breath.

What's wrong, ma? Are you okay? I asked, switching from my tranquil state to an alert one.

It hurt, Hanele, but I don't know vhat it is, she winced. *I tink it's noting* [nothing], *but I gonna lie down.*

I'm gonna call Dr. Klibanoff, ma. I'm worried about you.

Dr. Klibanoff advised me she could be having a gallstone attack and that I should get her to a hospital right away. More afraid than I had ever been, I left our apartment and ran to ask Mr. Sklarz whether he would take us to Springfield Hospital. One of the three fun-loving, handsome Sklarz brothers, I knew he had a new car and would be willing to drive us to the hospital. My mother was reluctant to leave our apartment to seek medical care. She was not willing to give in to a possible illness, which would take her away from her job and put our livelihood in jeopardy. The pain was so intense, she was forced to consent to my wishes.

Maria, one of my mother's cohorts at the Victoria Dress Corporation offered to care for me during the time my mother stayed in the hospital to have her gallbladder removed and recover from her ensuing yellow jaundice. In those days, hospital stays were much longer, and my mother's condition warranted a two-week visit. I recall I was in a more modern, spacious environment than one of the tiny apartments on Osgood Street, large enough that I was given my own bedroom.

That is when my fortnight of somnambulism apparently began, not that I personally recollected anything I did during my nighttime jaunts. Here is how one night was described to me:

Within an hour of retiring to sleep, I rose up from my bed and went out to the living room, where two people were watching television. Apparently, I then asked,

Did you see where Laura went? I've been looking for her.
The response: *No, I think you are dreaming. Let's get you back to bed.*
No, I said. *She asked me for toast. I told her I would try to find some for her, but I can't find any here. I just can't,* I added, tears in my eyes.
Let's see if we can get you back to sleep, Hanna.

No, I can't do that. I have to find some toast and bring it to her. She needs it.

I know, but we can't do that now. You need to go back to sleep.

Still weeping, I was led back to my bed and proceeded to fall directly asleep.

Similar scenes involving my mother's time in various concentration camps unfolded on subsequent nights. For instance, one night I was participating in a roll call at a concentration camp. On another night, I was burying a turnip under the nose of Nazi camp guards.

I had absorbed my mother's stories into my unconscious, and during her absence, I had reenacted some of them during my stint of sleepwalking. My search for toast related to an incident where my mother's sister Laura had asked for a piece of toast while they were both at the Bergen Belsen camp, the last camp in their year's journey of torture. My mother was always frustrated at not fulfilling her sister's one simple desire, just a slice of toast. Laura died of typhus soon after her feeble request, shortly before the British Second Army liberated the camp. My mother's frustration must have been inadvertently transferred to me without my even realizing it.

I believe my caretakers told my mother upon coming home from the hospital about my sleepwalking antics. If so, we certainly never spoke about it. Upon her discharge, she was already too busy planning an early return to her job, having missed more than two weeks with no pay. Despite her reluctance, she asked for financial assistance from the Jewish Social Service Bureau in order to pay for our food, rent, and utilities. Curiously, once I was back in our apartment with her, my need to express some of her horrible life events through my unconscious summarily ceased and never reoccurred. However, my mother's tortuous stories continued.

CHAPTER 21

Scenes From a Communal Life

We were just like most other children in many ways. Unless someone met our parents and heard their accents, or visited our refugee enclave on Osgood Street, we could pass for average American-born kids living in a neighborhood like any other. Speaking perfect English and exposed to such everyday cultural phenomena as comic books, hula-hoops, hopscotch, baseball, American history, and rock and roll, we fit right in with the rest of American society. Only we knew we were different.

The *grine* tended to have small families. Many had just one child, some two, and rarely, three. The small group of children in the community came to know one another well and often considered one another as family. Yet, we all felt as though we carried an intangible burden that was entirely inexplicable.

Among the children of the *grine*, Sally and Adina were my best friends. As small children, we played percussion on pots and pans for a while, thinking we sounded pretty good and requesting small donations as we roamed the various apartments and played our makeshift instruments for the tenants on Osgood Street. Later, Sally's father made us reluctantly return all the nickels and dimes we had collected since, in his opinion, we had earned the money under false pretense, that is, good entertainment. Sometimes Mayan, whose family eventually moved away when she was nine to own a general store on Long Island, joined us when we were a little older as we all read *Archie* comic books, played cards, or listened to records together. At other times, we danced to rock and roll records, where I played the male part owing to my rapidly increasing height.

My most audacious play activity, however, occurred with Sandra. She lived in the two-family house at the other end of Osgood Street near the cross section with Main. The apartment she shared with her mother was on the second floor and had only a small, unscreened outside porch. We often engaged in a bizarre and highly dangerous activity that entailed climbing up onto the railing of the porch and walking back and forth across it as though we were on a tightrope. One false step and we could have fallen onto the pavement below. The exhilaration of this adventure enticed us to continue doing it whenever her mother was not home.

All the *grine* children often roamed through each other's apartments as though they were extensions of their own homes, often to meet a friend. We kept a close eye on the everyday occurrences of the various families, at times observing more than we wanted to see, like disagreements between spouses or the discipline of the children.

Sometimes, as I passed through an apartment, I saw one of the men lying prone on his bed, naked from the waist up. As he lay there, his wife placed small, round, heated glass cups in rows on his back, as many as would fit. The suction from the heated cups allowed them to stay in place while the blood flowed to near the skin's surface. *He got such a bad cold*, Mrs. Zagruder said to me. *Da bankes* [cupping] *vill help to pull out da shlime* [phlegm].

When I returned to pass through the same apartment again, Mr. Zagruder, his small, half-naked body still lying straight on his bed, looked as though he had endured a rough boxing bout in which he had been knocked out and brought back to his room to recover. As he lay face down, his back was filled with blood-red marks from the rounded glass cups.

How do you feel, Mr. Zagruder? I asked.

Much better. I feel much better, he replied in a tired, nasal voice, turning his face to one side in order to speak.

Maybe it was a psychological effect, but it seemed to work. However, the sight of the multiple deep, red, round marks, prominent on his back, made me sick to my stomach. *I'm really glad,* I said, gagging. *I hope you feel all better soon.*

I remember most the aroma of the European Jewish cuisine that permeated the kitchens, invariably drawing my curiosity about what was on the stove or in the oven. Many of the children ate *gribenes* as an after-school snack. *Gribenes* were crispy chicken skins with onions, a byproduct of rendering chicken fat into *schmaltz,* spread on rye bread. My mother rarely made this delicacy, which was favored more by the Polish members of our community. Its savory fragrance in the numerous kitchens I visited, however, was enough to satisfy my appetite.

My mother, known more for her sewing than cooking talent, frequently made *kreplach,* akin to wonton, filled with ground meat or potatoes, on special holidays. So ubiquitous was the delicacy, I could have easily watched the same process of rolling out the dough into an exceedingly thin layer at any other apartment in my building. After cutting the dough into squares and placing the filling inside, the chefs of Osgood Street formed the dough into triangles and placed them into boiling water. My mother always used the brown-enamel cookware she had brought with her on the journey to America from Bergen Belsen for all her cooking, and this was no exception. I have always retained the image of water boiling in her enameled Dutch oven on the stove, ready for matzo balls, chicken fricassee, or kreplach. Although most of the time the finished product was included in chicken soup, I often ate one of the *kreplach* on its own and made it my meal.

Oy Hanele, you gonna eat my kreplach before ve have our soup?

Yeah, ma. I can't really wait for the soup. I have to have at least one now, and then I'll also have some in my soup.

You crazy, Hanele! she said with a smile, relishing my enjoyment of her rare cooking talent.

Often, the cooks among the *grine* adopted American recipes into their vast culinary repertoire:

Vhat's new today, Hanele? Mrs. Landsman always asked me with that illusory smile of hers on her face and did a little wiggle as soon as I walked into her apartment.

Are you here to see Yussie? He is sitting on the sofa in the living room if you vant to see him.

No, I'm here to see you. I heard you were making your mocha cream cake, and I wanted to see how you make it.

Okay. Vell, I am in da middle of making it now, so you can vatch if you vant to.

Yeah, I'll just stand here and watch you if you don't mind.

She used a jellyroll pan to make the yellow cake, which was just about to come out of the oven. Removing it, she gently turned over the pan and released the cake onto a clean towel and then rolled it up inside the towel. After letting it cool for a while, I watched as she unrolled the cake and spread the top with a mocha filling she had already prepared. Then she asked me,

Vould you like to roll da cake up again, Hanele? It's easy.

Oh, no, no, no. That's okay. I'm not a very good cook. Really, I'm just here to watch.

Okay, she replied with a little chuckle. *Next time you vill do it.*

She then expertly rolled the cake back up again and placed it in the refrigerator. Later, when she was ready to serve it, she would slice the cake roll to expose the swirls of delicious mocha cream on the inside.

> *You vill come after supper tonight and taste da cake, right Hanele?*
>
> *I can't wait.*

It was fun to watch this cooking lesson, but in my case, it was like the algebra I will never use in my real life. After watching the experts in cooking and sewing, I should have been a connoisseur of domesticity, but I never became much of a cook, like Mrs. Landsman, or a seamstress, like my mother — just an observer. Since my mother never asked me to participate in the preparation of either food or clothing, and I never asked, my lack of creative ability in these areas is little wonder.

Living on Osgood Street and working at low-paying jobs, the *grine* struggled to make ends meet, but they doted on their children, viewing them as extensions of their families into the future. They were willing to sacrifice anything for them. The future, a concept that only a few years before might not have been possible, meant everything to them.

They made sure their children were well fed and warmly dressed in the frigid New England winter, and they paid close attention to school grades. Although certain members of their community inflicted harsh punishments when their children disobeyed (as perhaps they had learned from their own parents in their youth), it did not deter them from placing all their hopes and dreams in their children. They were willing to use whatever skills they had to ensure their offspring lived happy, prosperous lives.

However, the *grine*'s tendency to keep important life secrets from their children in order to protect them from the horrors of their parents' past also deprived the children from knowing their parents' true nature. As with my mother, who protected the secret of my conception in a displaced persons camp, they developed patterns of secrecy constructed in our childhoods that continued into our adulthood. Indeed, their ever-present smiles, with the exception of my mother's taciturn visage, were skillful covers of inner torment. Each of them kept much of the terrifying portions of their lives to themselves until their deaths. Even so, their children instinctively felt their pain and spent their lifetimes protecting them from any undue grief and sorrow. In a reversal of roles, guarding our parents from any future unhappiness became a full-time responsibility.

When I returned to the Landsmans' apartment later that night to taste the mocha cream cake, no one was home. Turning away from their front door and then looking back again through their windows at the lonely darkness inside, I wondered why Mrs. Landsman had invited me if she and her family would not be there. The aroma of the mocha cake still swirled through my nostrils, making me yearn for just a nibble of the creamy confection. The thought of it was so intoxicating that I was not sure whether I could wait another day for the taste.

Returning to our apartment, I asked my mother whether she knew the whereabouts of the Landsmans.

Ikh veyse nisht [I don't know], *Hanele,* my mother replied to my question. *Maybe dey just vent out for an ice cream.*
It's kinda funny that they're not home when they invited me to come, I said. *It's really strange.*

Early the next morning before school, I decided to check again to see whether the Landsmans were home. Approaching their door, I knocked several times. Hearing no response, I was just about to turn around and leave, when finally, Mr. Landsman opened the door to greet me.

Hi, Chanele. Vhy you come so early?

I'm so glad you're home. Well, Mrs. Landsman invited me to come and taste her cake last night, but nobody was home, and I was wondering if everything was okay. Are you all okay?

Oy, now I remember. Rivkah told me she invite you to come for cake. But ve took her to da hospital last night. She lose da baby, you know, but she is feeling good. She vill be fine.

Okay, thanks for telling me. Please tell her I miss her and I hope she'll be back home soon, will you?

Yes, I vill tell her, but she vill be home in a few days and you can see her den.

I walked away thinking about Mrs. Landsman's cheerfulness only the day before, as she made that glorious mocha cake. Now that joy was erased by the loss of an unborn baby, whose life would have held such importance to a couple that had experienced more losses than any human beings should have to face. She never told me about her pregnancy, and I wondered whether anyone else knew. Most likely, she had not even confided the news about her expected child to her son. Like the rest of our community, she and her husband were hardened by their past, which gave them the strength and courage to cope with any new traumas that came their way. Moreover, they kept it all to themselves. Mrs. Landsman was never again able to conceive.

CHAPTER 22

Outings

The *grine* knew how to have fun. They yearned to enjoy life with their children to the fullest. Starting soon after their arrival in Springfield, they seemed to have a knack for finding the best outdoor spots in the city and its surroundings to picnic, to skate, to swim, to hike, to commune with nature, and just to take pleasure in the outdoors.

Five Mile Pond, on Boston Road, was chosen for swimming in the beginning. A spring-fed pond, five miles from Main Street (thus, its name), it was just a few minutes' drive from Osgood Street and featured a comfortable, clear swimming hole and beach area. We could often find a member of the *grine* who owned a car to pack several of us in the front and back seats for the summer jaunt to Boston Road.

My mother's natural olive-toned skin was prone to tanning even while sitting under an umbrella and fully clothed, but I had to be careful lest I burn to a crisp.

Vatch out, Hanele. Ve put on lotion, but don't svim out in da sun too long, my mother warned.

Okay, ma, I yelled from the water. But I usually had too much fun swimming with the other children to worry about any sunburn.

I'll show you how I can do a handstand in the water, I said to Adina, after seeing many of the children perform the acrobatic feat. It did not take me very long to put my underwater handstand on display. *This is easy*, I said to myself, not noted for possessing any other sporting talents, and certainly unable to perform this gymnastic stunt on land.

I can do one too. Watch me, Adina screamed.

All those on shore must have chuckled at the sea of children performing underwater handstands, their legs and feet shooting straight up above the water's surface. It was a skill that we continued to perfect when the *grine* ventured out to farther swimming spots in Ellington, Connecticut, south of Springfield, like Shady Lake and Crystal Lake.

Inevitably, when we returned home, my mother would be browner than ever, while she washed my skin down with vinegar to promote healing and prevent blisters on my sunburn. *You too long in da sun, Hanele. I told you to vatch out*, she chided each time.

Later into the 1950s, in the summertime, we joined a small group of *grine* who drove all the way out to Moodus, Connecticut, during the heyday of family resorts for longer vacations of a week or two. These days, I wonder how they ever found that vacation spot, easily more than an hour's drive from Osgood Street before parts of I–91, running north and south along the Connecticut River, had completed construction. They not only discovered it, they made detailed plans for lodging, meals, and sightseeing along the way.

Ve stop at Gillette Cestle, right? asked Mrs. Lakser, referring to the stone fortress castle situated high on a hill overlooking the Connecticut River and built by William Gillette, the actor famous for playing Sherlock Holmes on stage in the early twentieth century.

Of course, vu den [what else]? her husband answered.

What did the greenhorns know of William Gillette, or of Sherlock Holmes, for that matter? Maybe nothing, but they acted as though they were his biggest fans as they closely followed their roadmap to his mansion, like professional travelers. Like all the other tourists, we wandered the landscape at Gillette Castle, posing for photographs and walking along the tracks and over the bridges and into the tunnels of the three-mile, formerly private railroad on the property.

Sidonia, on the right, with friends at Gillette Castle, 1957

Already ten years old that first summer in Moodus, I caused my share of melodrama, proving that the attachment between my mother and me was even tighter than anyone had suspected. Despite my nagging ambivalence toward her, I still maintained my fear of losing her if I were to let her out of my sight for too long.

My mother, however, could afford to take only one week off from her work at the Victoria Dress Corporation in 1957, even though some of the women could be off for another week. She pleaded with me to stay another week in the care of one of the other ladies, but I could not bear to see her depart when she was driven back by one of the men who also needed to return to work.

Please, ma, I begged, as I grasped her arm. *I want to go home too. I can't stay here without you. Please don't leave me.*

Oy Hanele, you vill be happy here anoder veek mit your friends, she explained by the pool.

I looked at the pool, an enticing feature for a ten-year-old girl, and then looked back at her, and looked at the pool again. Making much more of a scene than I realized at the time, while everyone around the pool watched and wondered how this drama would end, I finally gave in to my mother's wishes.

Okay, ma. I'll stay if you really want me to, I said, amid my sobs.

After kissing me goodbye, she walked away as I held on to her leg, causing her to walk stiff-legged to the waiting car. I cried until the car drove away and I could no longer see her head in the back seat.

By the following summer, when we returned to the Moodus resort for our vacation, I had the previous year's experience behind me when I had thoroughly enjoyed the second week without my mother. That next year, staying on the second week without her proved to be a much simpler task. *I can't believe I made such a big deal last year,* I said to myself this time, feeling a great deal more grown up.

CHAPTER 23

The Card Counter

Card games tend to bring out aspects of one's character, sometimes beneficent and sometimes onerous, that might never otherwise be observed. Good fortune regarding which cards are dealt to each player is an important factor. However, even more important to an individual's success at cards is the precise employment of strategy. What kind of strategy players choose can be the deciding factor in whether they reach the heights of victory or the gloom of defeat, and whether they can live with themselves afterward.

The card players among the *grine* took every opportunity to sit down together to play a game of cards. In the process, they acquired an intimate knowledge of the manner in which each of them approached the competition. Some players were careless in their bets and did not make wise decisions about which cards they discarded or kept. Others were overly serious about the game and quick to accuse a fellow player of foul play if things did not go their way. Still others played more for the camaraderie than the competition and easily went along with the outcome, win or lose.

It took a little while for the male players to come to a deduction about one of their colleagues who won a little too consistently. The conclusion: one player among them had a special advantage. Mr. Liskowitz was a card counter.

A player is counting cards when he closely studies the cards played and based on what he sees, he assigns a point value to each card. In the process of the game, he keeps a running tally of the cumulative value of the cards in his head to assist him in determining his wager and to minimize his risk of losing. Since I was not familiar with the games enjoyed by the card-playing group, I could not say how Mr. Liskowitz's counting obsession actually worked in their particular game. As a budding card player myself, however, I was somewhat familiar with the phenomenon and understood how annoying and frustrating it must have been to watch the scene unfold on various occasions.

Mr. Liskowitz began to win games, one after the other, to the amazement of his fellow competitors and good friends. Grinning and rolling his eyes, he seemed to gain immense satisfaction after a supposedly fortuitous win. A usually serious, solemn man with steely, mournful eyes and slicked-back dark hair, he seemed rather bland when I saw him on non-card-playing occasions. Yet his face changed dramatically when he was participating in a game and especially if he pulled out a win. Interestingly, the wagers were small amounts, usually in the nickel range. A win barely enhanced the pockets of any player, so Mr. Liskowitz's aim was not to get rich but rather to satisfy his competitive need to win.

No one knew whether his counting was a habit acquired early in life, requiring no conscious thought, or whether his counting was a deliberate offensive tactic. Perhaps it was a strategic approach to life, something he had learned in surviving the Holocaust, staying ahead of his opponents. Either way, he had to be stopped. His buddies decided to use a series of delicate, tactful approaches to thwart Moyshe Liskowitz. Their first attempt entailed bombarding him with conversation so he would lose his concentration.

Moyshe, so how is your vork going? Are you busy at da factory? asked the dealer.

Oy, ve are very busy. I sometime put in extra hours to finish my vork.

An how is your vayb [wife]? *I heard she got a job vit a dress factory last veek,* commented another player.

She is fine, Mr. Liskowitz responded.

An deine tokhter [your daughter]? *Vhat's going on in school? Is she a klige kind* [smart child]? *Somevon told me she vas very smart. Vhat do you tink?* asked yet another player.

Vell, yeh, she is klig. School? I don't know. I mean, yes, I do know. She is good, Mr. Liskowitz responded, overwhelmed by the flurry of questions.

Dat's good. My son bring home bad marks from school last time, so ve are vatching him to do his homevork. How is your tokhter vit homework? She vill read better den you. Do you tink so?

As the conversation to distract Mr. Liskowitz continued, he became increasingly irritated, but his game was barely affected. He still maintained his ability to focus and count cards, and therefore, win. The other players were beginning to think that stopping Mr. Liskowitz's card-counting ways was a hopeless case. *Er vet baytn vi a toytn bankes,* I heard someone say. (Trying to get him to change is as futile as blood-cupping a corpse.) They came to the conclusion they would have to combine their tactics with something else or replace them with a more effective scheme to deter his efforts.

Mr. Landsman went home after one game and told his wife about the group's frustration at the card-counting fiasco.

Oy, ikh hob shoyn tsores genig [I have enough troubles already], Mr. Landsman complained to his wife. *Vhy he playing dis vay?*

She had some advice for him: *Mr. Stern should be da first dealer. He is very fast vit cards. Maybe if he deal da cards so fast, Moyshe von't have a chance to count. Try it.*

Okay. Vhat could be bad? It's vort [worth] a try, he said, *shrugging his shoulders.*

Mr. Stern grabbed the deck at the next game and dealt the cards as swiftly as he could, knowing he still would not have control over the players' decisions about which cards they picked up or discarded. But, combined with exhaustive conversation, it seemed to deter Mr. Liskowitz a little bit. After a while, they also began to recognize his waging patterns, rising and falling at times to match certain played cards. In other words, they attempted to learn some counting techniques themselves in order to foil the counter.

I observed Mr. Liskowitz playing with the card players for as long as I lived with them on Osgood Street. He was never expelled from the group for his card-counting tricks. His friends had curbed his habit enough to tolerate his style of play. After all, their mutual friendship meant more than the win of a few nickels.

CHAPTER 24

The Matchmaker: Progress Report 2

After Mr. Goodman's marriage, only four of the bachelors remained as potential mates for my mother. The stress of trying to curry favor with them as much as possible was almost overwhelming. It was a relief to observe that one of them, Mr. Zwillen, the one who evoked my intense fear, seemed to be preoccupied with another woman.

My mother and I used to walk everywhere we wanted to go, except when we took the city bus to downtown Springfield. Upon occasion, when we could not afford to pay the bus fare, we ventured the long walk from the North End through the crowded urban streets to downtown and back. Our urgency to travel to the commercial part of the city usually coincided with the completion of one of my mother's sewing creations. Most of the time, if we had money left over at the end of the month after expenses and savings, we spent it on sewing notions and accessories, like matching buttons, to complement my mother's designs. For example, a skirt might need a matching sweater, socks, or purse — items that we usually purchased at such small boutique stores as Muriels, Brighams, or the upscale Casual Corner — all downtown. Sometimes, while we were there, we wandered around the vast multifloor department store, Forbes and Wallace, and purchased a household item.

Many of the things we needed for our everyday existence were located within the six-block area of Dwight Street, from Calhoun to Ringgold Street, three blocks north and three blocks south of Osgood. We walked up and down that small portion of Dwight Street, along with the rest of the *grine* and everyone else who lived in our apartment building, almost every day.

One summer morning, as we took our walk to Chernick's Kosher Meat Market to purchase some *pulkes* (chicken drumsticks) to roast, I noticed Mr. Zwillen was close behind us. I could hear his loud, gruff voice over my head, talking to someone who was walking beside him. Ahead, we could already see the group of *grine* men gathered together in front of the butcher shop, their usual meeting place to congregate and talk, laugh, and smoke together.

> *I think Mr. Zwillen is behind us ma,* I whispered, rising up on my toes to meet her chin, my growth spurt still ahead of me.
> *Don't look back, Hanele. Ve just gonna valk straight like ve don't know he is dere,* my mother replied, grabbing my hand.
> *Someone else is walking with him, a woman,* I said.
> *Yeh, his new girlfriend,* she said with a snicker.
> *I didn't know he had one.*
> *Yeh, tank Got.*

So Mr. Zwillen had a new girlfriend. As I secretly peeked out of the corner of my eye to take a closer look, I realized that I did not recognize her. When I heard her voice, though, I noticed she had some kind of accent, but she was not part of my refugee group. I had no idea where Mr. Zwillen had met her or from what neighborhood she came.

She was fairly attractive, but in a plain sort of way. She had straight brown hair pulled back with barrettes on either side of her head and wore pink lipstick along with what looked like eyebrow pencil. Wearing a solid-brown cotton skirt and white short-sleeved blouse, her body looked pretty muscular and athletic.

Let go fun [from] *my arm. You sqveezing me too hard,* I heard her say to him.

Okay, sorry, he replied rather sheepishly. Since I was still facing forward, I assumed he had withdrawn his hand from her arm.

Dat's better. I am not a shopping bag! the mystery woman said. Her voice sounded firm and assertive as though she would not stand for anyone pushing her around. I was glad Mr. Zwillen had found someone who was not a pushover, someone who would not crumble at his fiery temper.

As we approached the gathered men in front of Chernick's, I could hear their howls and quips about Mr. Zwillen having a new lady friend. My mother and I ignored the whole scene and walked right into the store after saying our quick hellos. Once inside, I finally looked up at my mother and noticed she had a rare grin on her face. *Vhat you have today for pulkes, Mr. Chernick?* she asked, as though the whole incident had never occurred.

CHAPTER 25

Patterns and Styles

I wish I had saved all my mother's homemade creations. I should have built more closets to house the fashions representing the evolution of her patterns and styles, some reflecting changing times, but most a revelation of her incremental skill at innovation and design. Instead, I have to settle for the garments she created over just the last twenty years of her life.

When we first moved to Osgood Street in the early 1950s, my mother had already exhibited her talent on a few notable occasions. In honor of Mrs. Alpert's announcement of her impending marriage and our departure from her home, she made the first of her business suits for me, even though I was just four years old. The black-and-white wool check suit with tailored collar and cuffs and matching pleated skirt was an early masterpiece — a harbinger of the business suits I wore twenty years later.

Even our visa photographs indicate my mother's budding talent at creative expression, although in a simplified way. Her photograph shows her wearing a homemade stone-brown wool coat with stiff shoulder pads. Mine reveals a toddler's dark wool jumpsuit buttoned down the side. It was obvious she had sewn both garments, and had probably honed her craft a little, in the displaced persons camp where she lived for four years during the time we had posed for the visa pictures. When she was asked at Camp Wentorf, the visa processing camp near Hamburg, Germany, what her profession would be to ensure she would not become a public charge in America, she replied "seamstress." That one spur-of-the-moment response proved to be a prophecy for the rest of her life.

Sewing was like breathing to her. Although she had known how to sew since her childhood, she was not considered an expert. Sewing was necessary for clothing a rural family. According to my mother, the real experts were her sisters and her mother, who was considered the best needle pointer in the area.

Novon vas better den my moder mit a needle, she often told me.

I don't know, ma. You can really sew too, I invariably replied.

No, not like dem. Not like dem, Hanele.

In Hungary, the women's attire reflected the agrarian nature of their environment, often a plain long skirt, shirt, and coat. In addition, their orthodox Jewish faith dictated that the women dress modestly, covering their arms and legs, and in my grandmother's case, her hair. The opportunity to dress up in finer garments in their small world was nonexistent.

Coming to America opened up a brand-new universe of fashion and modernity unknown in my mother's birthplace. She soaked it up like a sponge. One person was always available to try out her new fashion ideas, inspired by magazines, television, and simply by observing Americans walking on the street — me. My lean physique suited her creative aspirations perfectly. In many ways, I have often felt I was an experiment in more than just the fashion sense, but in a broader sense. I provided a daily practice lesson of how to parent a child who comes unexpectedly into one's own in a new world, with no experience or help from anyone.

PORT OF **NEW YORK, N. Y.**
I certify that the immigrant named herein arrived in the United States at this port on the

S. S. USAT **"GENERAL R. L. HOWZE"**

on **JUL 3 1949**

and was inspected by me and duly admitted ~~held for SI~~

under Section 3 B of the Immigration Act of **JUN 25 1948**

JUL 3 1949   *Immigrant Inspector.*

0203 K-3845
JAN 5 1950   **RECORD OF BSI**
The immigrant named herein was ~~admitted~~ ~~excluded and appeal granted.~~

Date

                                        Chairman BSI.

                RECORD OF APPEAL
Admitted   Excluded   Date

SIDONIA PERLSTEIN

☐ Nonquota; Subdivision (   ) Section 4

☐ Nonpreference; Quota ....   **P.L. 774**

☐ First preference; Quota ....

☐ Second preference; Quota ....

☒ Hungarian .. Seamstress .. Section 6b . Public Law 774

IMMIGRATION VISA No. *486/51*

American Foreign Service

at **Hamburg (Wentorf), Germany**   Date **26 MAY 1949**

SEEN: Szidonia **PERLSTEIN** *642*   The bearer

who is of **Hungarian**   (Citizen or subject)

Nationality, having been seen and examined, is classified as a **Displaced Person** immigrant and is granted this Immigration Visa pursuant to the Immigration Act of 1924, as amended, and **Public Law 774**

The validity of this Immigration Visa expires 4 months from date of issue .... otherwise noted.

Fee No. *1949*
~~Fee of~~ No fee prescribed   *Ralph G. Clark*
Vice-Consul .... of the
United States of America.

Passport No.   or other travel document
Passport waived by Secretary of State under date September 28, 1948   (Describe)
Issued to

Issued by

Date
Valid until

NOTE.—This Immigration Visa will not entitle the person to whom issued to enter the United States if upon arrival in the United States he is found to be inadmissible to the United States under the immigration laws. (Sub-division (g), sec. 2, Immigration Act of 1924.)

Sidonia's document certifying arrival at the port of New York, July 3, 1949, "Occupation: seamstress"

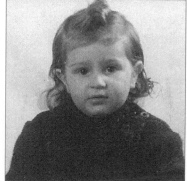

The author and her mother's visa photos, 1949

Stand up straight was my mother's motto for fashion and life. *Stand up straight or else I gonna have a crooked hem. I don't tink you vant a crooked hem, right?*

Sometimes I felt like saying, *Yeah, I wouldn't mind a crooked hem if I didn't have to stand here fitting for so long.* But mostly, I just whined, *Do I have to?* As a committed nonsewer myself, I never could commiserate with the sewer's need for cooperation from the model in perfecting the fit of a garment.

On Osgood Street, my mother crafted hundreds of garments at home and many more at the Victoria Dress Corporation, which specialized in ladies casual fashions. Since female students were not permitted to wear pants to school then, she sewed mainly skirts, blouses, and shirtwaist dresses for my everyday attire. Never possessing the patience to work on any single piece for too long, she acquired the talent of completing garments in record time while maintaining strict accuracy.

Her need for speed was assisted by adding an electric motor to her sewing machine to replace the use of the much slower foot treadle. An unwillingness to stop making buttonholes by hand in favor of using a modern buttonhole machine still did not slow down her typically rapid pace of production. The astounding result allowed me to showcase different garments at school and at play with few repetitions. Meanwhile, my mother wore only a few simple homemade skirts and dresses, which downplayed her figure and avoided any onlooker's gaze.

In part because of my rapid growth and partly because of my mother's prolific output, my clothes often had to be given away to charity. We never had adequate closet space to accommodate so many.

Indeed, my wardrobe in the 1950s laid the foundation for my mother's later show pieces. It included plaid pleated skirts with

The author, wearing a homemade jumper, with her mother in a dress she fashioned, around 1958

matching jackets; polka-dot skirts and dresses in a variety of contrasting colors; cotton pastel-colored shirtwaist dresses in various sleeve lengths; jumpers with matching long-sleeved blouses; wide twirling poodle skirts covering several layers of petticoats; and wool and cotton fitted pants. Most of the outfits were accompanied by my white-and-black saddle shoes or brown loafers, purchased during our trips to downtown Springfield. My entire collection of garments reflected the talents of a rural Hungarian woman who had easily adapted to the modern styles of a new land.

While my mother was already creating her one-of-a-kind fashions in the 1950s, she also began to develop a pattern of reclusiveness and isolation in order to safeguard her inscrutable history. Her creativity was on full display, but her real emotions remained inside.

CHAPTER 26

Nerves

My heart was pounding really fast. When I was eight years old and started the fourth grade at public school, I began to notice it more and more. No longer in the insular environment of the Lubavitcher Yeshiva, my exposure to other adults and children outside my refugee community became considerably wider. The slightest confrontation with events beyond my normal experience would stir up the quickened pace of my heartbeat.

Sometimes the thought of an impending school exam sent me into a tailspin, a common response experienced by many school-children. At times, I felt out of place and nervous with the other children of the *grine*, not having the same kind of family composition as they did. If they had ever asked me about my father, I would not have known how to answer. Although, luckily, none of them ever did, I was always expecting the question to arise. At other times, the fear of merely having to kick a ball during my physical education class caused me to freeze before the ball, unable to initiate the proper brain signals to my feet, which incurred the snickers of my classmates.

Are you going to stand there forever or are you going to kick it? The name of the game is "kickball" you know, a boy in my class often yelled out to me, while my other classmates giggled.

I know. I'm gonna kick it, I replied miserably, not looking back at him, just staring down at my feet. When I finally kicked the ball, it was a limp, aimless stroke that just made an already embarrassing situation worse.

My mother had entertained me with stories of her prowess as a gifted ball handler and jumper in her youth, but she never taught me anything about those feats. Lacking anyone else to teach me the techniques, I never learned how to kick or throw a ball. They were foreign skills to me, provoking intense, unbridled anxiety and preventing me from fully participating in most sports.

My efforts to initiate interest from the bachelors in my refugee community on behalf of my mother were also beginning to take their toll on my psyche, although it did not stop me from continuing in my efforts. The frustration of attempting to incur their favor created a brewing storm in my belly and heart.

By the time I was ten, having listened for five years to my mother's harrowing tales of the Holocaust combined with her tranquil remembrances of a family that no longer existed, I had unconsciously incorporated the stories as part of my own consciousness. As evidenced by my brief period of somnambulism, when I enacted some of her frightening memories, it was often difficult to differentiate between my mother's accounts of her past and my present-day existence. The trauma of hearing those sagas created its own set of insidious fears.

My greatest source of anxiety was assuredly my ongoing uncertainty about the circumstances of my birth and the mystery about my father. I often wondered why my mother could not tell me about him. What could have occurred at the time of my conception that prevented her from confiding in me? How could she be so cruel as to hide such important details from her own daughter, the only other member of her family?

She had created an environment of secrecy that thwarted at every turn any thoughts of confronting her and asking her those questions. I frequently thought that I had worked up the nerve to ask her, when each time, her sober expression and her invisible roadblocks deterred me. Trying to suppress my anger at her was a full-time endeavor that created a mountain of angst. Was there anyone else in the world who was experiencing the same circumstances? I thought not.

So, while only ten years old, I began to think of myself as someone with a "nervous" disorder. Although I could not always target what had caused my nervousness at any given moment, my fast heartbeat and muddled brain seemed to remain with me. I wondered who, if anyone, might be the right person with whom to share my worries about my mental state.

I decided that Rabbi Moses Sheinkopf, the rabbi at the Russische Shul and the principal of my afternoon Hebrew School, would be the right person to listen to my concerns. Perhaps he could give me some guidance about how to handle this most disconcerting state of mental affairs. He seemed to be a serious, wise man with a commanding, noble bearing, giving the impression of someone whose life was thoroughly in order. He may have been in his fifties at that time, often wearing a dark suit and coat with a fedora. With a dark brown mustache and a well-groomed, pointed goatee on his chin, rather than a full beard, he was obviously a prominent man in Jewish society. In fact, I had heard that he was the chief orthodox rabbi in Springfield. A distinguished man like that, I figured, must have some sage advice to share with me.

Seeking him out one day after my Hebrew class, I found him as he was about to leave the building and embark on a walk to his next appointment.

Rabbi Sheinkopf, can I walk with you? I just have some things on my mind, and I thought maybe you could help, I began.

Of course, Hanele. We can walk and talk at the same time if you don't mind, he responded.

Okay. That's fine with me, I replied as we began to walk together.

So what's on your mind? he asked.

It's hard to know where to start, I said, wondering whether I was doing the right thing by talking with him.

You can start anywhere, even in the middle if you want, he remarked, trying to allay my obvious nervousness.

Well, I've been feeling kind of weird lately, like I am always afraid, but I don't usually know why. Sometimes I can wake up and feel okay, but by the end of the day, I just feel unsure about everything. I'm afraid of starting to cry in front of my friends for no reason. I was wondering if you could give me some advice on how to feel better.

Can you think of any reason why you might feel this way?

No, I'm really not sure, I responded.

In part, my response was the truth. As with most children, I was not aware of all the sources of my stress. My mother's secrecy and her terrifying stories, my feelings of inadequacy with my school friends and playmates, the frustration of seeking a husband for her and a father for me — these were just the banal features of my everyday life. I was not fully conscious of their impact on my mental state. Yet, underneath it all, I knew these factors were not the normal features of a child's existence, but I could not bring myself to articulate them with the rabbi.

Well, you know, there is a saying in the Torah, he commented, *which says that when your heart has concerns, they may weigh you down, but a kind word will lift you up. Maybe you need more kind words to lift your fear, Hanele.*

Where can I get them, rabbi?

To begin with, I will be one of those who gives you the kind words. When I see you again, I will say some of the things I could have said before — about your devotion to your Hebrew studies, your fashionable appearance, and the good behavior your mother has instilled in you. For such a young girl, you are a mentsh [an honorable person] *already.*

I would love that. Thanks, rabbi, I said, as our walking paths took us in different directions.

The rabbi kept his promise through the years and always had a kind word for me when we met. It helped a bit to lift my spirits, even though my anxiety continued to plague me. He had not totally allayed my fears, but his words stayed with me for the rest of my life. I had grown to admire him so much that I chose him a dozen years later to officiate at my wedding.

CHAPTER 27

The Brownie

I never knew much about the appearance of any of my ancestors. Living in a small hamlet in the early twentieth century, where cameras were scarce, my mother's family never had their photographs taken. My imagination had to compensate for the lack of their exact images.

Using my mother's depictions of the personalities and characters of her siblings and parents, I tried to match the descriptions with what I thought they might look like. I imagined her brother, Dezso, as a tall, slim, wiry man with dark hair and a sly glint in his eye, as though he had just completed one of his daring adventures. Her oldest sister, Szeren, was a tall, elegant woman, wearing glasses, possibly resulting from her obsessive reading habit. Her sister Etel was a quiet, serene, content-looking woman with a comforting smile. The beautiful Laura was a bit shorter than the rest but possessed striking blue eyes, blond hair, and rosy cheeks, despite wearing no makeup. Simon, my mother's father, was a distinguished-looking man with silver gray hair and a silver beard. Hani, her mother, was tall and pretty, with chapped skin on her hands. Much of her face was hidden by a scarf, and her body was covered by her coat.

I even tried to imagine my mother's sister Margit, who had died of the Spanish flu pandemic after World War I, when my mother was only five years old. The memory of Margit had been treasured and discussed so often among my mother's family that my mother felt as though she knew her well. In turn, I felt the same way, imagining her as a studious, serious-faced teenager with intense hazel eyes and a rarely seen soft smile.

My mother's keen memory of her lost family had to suffice in passing on the fact of their existence to me and to future generations. However, in America, by the 1950s, most families owned a camera to capture the images of their children, their neighborhoods, such life events as weddings and other milestones, and trips and vacations. After our purchase of a television set, we decided that a simple camera, with no fancy accessories, was an essential item to own. Many of the *grine* had already obtained cameras and had snapped numerous pictures at their frequent parties and events.

It was an exciting day when we bought our Brownie Hawkeye Flash Camera for $5.50. We began to experiment with the black plastic boxlike device immediately. I do not remember ever having purchased a flash attachment, and we took most of our photos outside. Someone with a flash may have at times attached it to our camera and taken indoor shots. An easy camera for those of us with no technical knowledge, it allowed me to take quite a few photographs on the corner of Dwight and Osgood Streets or in front of the little Russische shul or at nearby Calhoun Park. At times, my mother and I asked someone to take our picture standing together in front of a street sign or in someone's backyard.

No focus or zoom mechanism was required. We just held the camera at waist height, looked down into the viewfinder on top of it to determine the desired image, and held our breath as we pressed down with our thumb on the shutter lever to the right. We turned the dial to wind the film for the next frame, and that was it. When we completed the roll of film, which held only ten to twelve shots, we walked over to Shankman's Pharmacy to develop our photographs, waiting about a week for their return. Sometimes when we viewed our developed roll of film, we were alarmed by the fuzziness of the images.

The Brownie Hawkeye camera

See ma, I told you that you had to hold the camera steady when you pressed the button. I think you must have moved, I said, even though I really had no idea what might have caused the blurry shots.

Oy, dat's right. I shouldn't breade (breathe) vhen I take da picture. Now I remember.

Our camera traveled with us everywhere we went. I usually held it by its short strap, which was affixed securely to its top, and swung it around as though it were a small lunch pail. When I look at the square black-and-white images we took back in the 1950s, I realize how important they were to my mother and her cohorts among the *grine*. They proved to be the permanent record of faces and places from our childhood that most of them had not possessed of their own childhood. I hope that the rest of the *grine* were as talented as my mother at storytelling so their offspring could learn as much as I did about family members they had not known.

The camera was a wonderful addition to the chronicling of our lives in America. Yet, despite its irrefutable value, sometimes it was no better than the combination of an active imagination and articulate description. Recent information from the United States Holocaust Museum about two of my mother's siblings, the only ones who lived long enough to have their characteristics described in Nazi questionnaires, provided examples of this phenomenon. As I perused the files pertaining to my Aunt Laura and Uncle Dezso during their journey through the Holocaust, I found the precise descriptions of both of them recorded by the Nazis as they entered various internment camps.

My Aunt Laura was five feet three inches tall and had a round face with blue eyes and light brown hair. Uncle Dezso was five feet eight and one half inches tall, with dark brown hair and a slender face and body. Despite his being shorter than I had anticipated (although he may have seemed taller to my mother in her childhood since he was thirteen years older), my imagination had captured his and Aunt Laura's images almost perfectly.

I just wish they had lived long enough for me to see them in person, to speak with them, and to get to know and love them as members of my family. It would have been worth an infinite number of cameras.

CHAPTER 28

The Matchmaker: Progress Report 3

The bachelors seemed to be pairing up with women really quickly by the mid-50s. Soon after Mr. Goodman had married his Jewish American bride, I noticed that Mr. Messinger was keeping company with a woman. She was not especially pretty, having a tall, lanky form and frizzy, short, dark hair. Yet her smile was wide and blissful, revealing a mouthful of teeth and gums enhanced by her dark red lipstick. I found myself looking forward to seeing her at some of our community gatherings.

Mr. Messinger seemed to have a permanent smile on his face, his eyes gleaming when he was by her side. Although she towered over him, she also seemed to diminish his gruff, sometimes disheveled appearance. He had taken to wearing an array of colorful bow ties, each cinched around his neck. They softened his features and gave him an aura of alacrity and contentedness. An American-born woman, perhaps from Boston or from one of those towns on the other side of the state (judging by her accent), his female friend sounded quite articulate, probably a product of higher education. She struck me as someone in her mid-thirties, much too old for a lady to remain unmarried. I imagined one of the matchmakers among the *grine* had met her and decided to introduce her to a bachelor in our community.

Chanele, did you meet my beautiful friend, Rose? Mr. Messinger asked me at Yussie's birthday party.

I saw her from far away, I said and, turning to her, *You have a great smile. You must be a happy person.*

Yes. Right now, I am very happy. Thanks for the compliment, she replied.

I was genuinely glad that Mr. Messinger had found someone who clearly was a good match for him. If a woman could light up a man's eyes and change his appearance so significantly just by her presence, I was all for it. Since I had never considered Mr. Messinger as the right partner for my mother, I was not too distressed by his loss as a contender for her hand. Yet, he was still one of my favorites among my identified bachelors. He deserved to be happy.

Mr. Messinger and his newfound love eventually married and had two sons together, but I lost track of them and never knew how their lives had evolved afterward. Mrs. Landsman, who had provided both Mr. Goodman and Mr. Messinger with hearty, homemade, daily meals, went back to serving only her husband and son.

Mr. Stossel and Mr. Olchinski were the only two who remained of the original bachelors who might have served as a husband for my mother and father figure for me. Time was running out for me to secure the paternal presence I so desired.

Part Three: Revelations

CHAPTER 29

The Somber Romantic

If there were ever a romantic bone in my mother's body, I certainly never saw it. She always exhibited little emotion in my youth. I never saw her go out on a date with a man or enter into any relationship with a member of the opposite sex. It would have been a surprise to me had she ever spoken about anyone in a romantic manner. As far as I was concerned, she could have been asexual.

Just because I never saw it does not mean she did not experience it — either the emotion or the relationship. When I discovered the cache of letters and photographs in her apartment upon moving her to elderly housing when she was eighty-five years old, I was intrigued by the following letter, written on thick paper with the letterhead of the *National Socialist German Worker Party* (the Nazi Party) *Reich Administration*. A subtitle under the main heading reads, *Office for Lottery Affairs*. The partially ripped and faded yellowing letter does not begin with any salutation. In other words, it is addressed to no one. Written in Yiddish, the English reads:

> *A man who has healthy legs doesn't consider it of any value. He knows very well that he is a Bohemian — oh, but I could also give you a horse with a donkey, as such a person gets a little bit of love. He goes into a tavern and drinks a glass of wine.*
>
> *A handsome officer, a young cavalier, dances with a young woman at a ball. They dance so feverishly until the perspiration*

runs down their faces in rivulets. They leave the dance hall to go outside. They kiss, they love one another, until finally they fall into a passionate ecstasy. [Read] between the lines — I shall end here since you are clever. Figure out the ending.

One year later, the officer happens to return to the same hotel. He sees that which he has lost — a woman with a child at her breast. He goes to her and asks her, "Who did this to you?" She answers with a downcast face, "It must have been from the glass of wine. . . . It was done in the excitement of life — all of the blood, the glass of wine."

Bergen Belzen [sic], 1945, IX, 10 (September 10, 1945)
Jacob Jackowitz

An even shorter letter appears on the flip side, apparently written by the same lovesick person and addressed to no one:

I haven't closed an eye all night, only thinking of you, my dear love. That was the most beautiful night that I spent with you, dear child. When you leave me, it hurts me so much. A terrible pain falls upon me because I am alone. Are you not happy with me? Let him love you better. I love you. I have time. I can wait. I haven't closed an eye all night and only thought of you, of you my dear child.

I have hope.

1945, IX, 10 (September 10, 1945) Bergen Belzen [sic] Camp
Jacob Jackowitz

It is unlikely these two letters were written to my mother since September 10, 1945, was only five months after she was liberated from the Bergen Belsen concentration camp. It does not make sense that she would have been involved in such an intense relationship so quickly — but I could be wrong. The year before the letters were written, she was imprisoned in three concentration camps, Auschwitz, Dachau, and finally Bergen Belsen, making her unavailable for a love affair, and impossible for her to have given birth by the date mentioned. Why then were these letters tucked among her collection of personal documents if they were not meant for her?

I had so many questions about the writer when I read those letters. He seems to have written the first letter in an allegorical manner, expressing his broken heart as a kind of morality tale filled with poignant metaphors referring to blood and wine and life and love. He interjects an observation pertaining to the mating of a horse and donkey as though they were humans participating in "a little bit of love." Perhaps he fancied himself as a cunning writer who conveyed his emotional state to the world, or to anyone who might examine his words, advising, "Read between the lines — I shall end here since you are clever. Figure out the ending." He writes this as though he were speaking directly to the person who is reading his little soliloquy, challenging her to imagine the ending scene of his night of love.

Since the letter refers to "a handsome officer, a young cavalier," could the writer have been a German officer? It is doubtful that a German officer would have been at Bergen Belsen on the date of the letters, September 10, 1945. Those remaining in the concentration camp after its liberation were moved a mile and a half away into former German army quarters and became residents of the Bergen Belsen displaced persons camp after April 15, 1945. Jewish Holocaust survivors became the main residents of the camp.

It was probably a Jewish survivor then who wrote the letters on the only stationery available at the time, about someone he had met before the war or soon thereafter. Could he have been dreaming the romantic relationship described in the letters, writing them in a fictional spirit? But then there is the reference to the "officer" one year later seeing "that which he has lost — a woman with a child at her breast." The similarity to my mother's circumstances in Bergen Belsen is eerily coincidental. Was my mother in a relationship with someone soon after her liberation? And were both letters, the officer's cautionary tale and the heartsick letter, referring to the sender not closing "an eye all night," meant for her?

It is also possible that the letters were intended for one of my mother's roommates at the Bergen Belsen displaced persons camp, where two or three women shared a room. Somehow, it may have found its way among her possessions. Striking a chord with her own situation, she may have hidden it from the intended recipient and kept it for herself.

All the possibilities regarding the two-sided letter were fascinating, but in the end, I found it did not make any difference to me whether the letters had been written to my mother or to someone else. The woman I had always viewed as somber and dispassionate had saved the letters and considered them important enough to hold on to for the rest of her life. Either she wanted to save the remnant of a romantic involvement she did not wish to forget, or perhaps the words of the letters just resonated in her heart. The letters served to show me that my mother possessed romantic emotions just as most people did. She was not the totally sullen, distant person she had displayed to the world.

Reading those letters so many years later made me wonder why, as a child, I had always thought my mother might be interested only in the bachelors among the *grine*. It never dawned on me to think she could ever be involved with another man, perhaps an American, someone who was not a part of our immigrant community. Working at the Victoria Dress Corporation, she was exposed to a number of men who were workers and managers in the textile business. Although she never would have shared it with me, she may have had feelings for another man, and that may have been why she never paid much attention to the bachelors on whom I had focused so much of my energy.

However, the most likely scenario was that my mother was never interested in a romantic relationship at all after her initial unsuccessful attempt. As I learned much later when translating her pile of documents, she may have been too fearful of repeating the mistake she had made with my father. After I read those other letters, I knew she had entered into an involvement resulting in a child with a much younger man, a teenager, a relationship doomed from the start. Influenced by his family and others, my young father decided to abandon my mother and his child once he emigrated from the displaced persons camp. His name was not the same as the signer of the love letters.

Desolate and lonely in the aftermath of World War II, she sought solace from a young man, another survivor in a displaced persons camp, one who may have offered her warmth and affection. When the romance did not result in a long-term commitment or marriage, she decided to keep the baby they had produced anyway. So hurt by those scornful events, she may have never lost the pain of a broken promise, never allowing herself to be so vulnerable again. To me, this latter notion seemed the most probable.

The letterhead of the romantic letter

CHAPTER 30

The Matchmaker: Progress Report 4

Mister Stossel looked up from his walk and saw me across Dwight Street. He gave me a wave with a toss of his hand, shouting, *Hi, Hanele.*

I waved back, *Where are you going, Mr. Stossel?*
To pick up some corn beef an pickles at Klibanoff's [delicatessen], he replied.
My favorite food, I shouted.

Usually his humped back forced him to continue looking down at the pavement, but occasionally, he stretched his neck and glanced up at whoever was walking near him or to observe passing cars. Because all that seemed to require a good deal of effort, I had few opportunities to talk to him as I had that day, unless we were seated together at a gathering inside our apartment building. Sometimes I wondered how someone with such a noticeable hump on his back could have survived the tortures of the Holocaust. If my mother's stories about the numerous "selections" were true, surely his deformity would have marked him for death, but he had made it out alive. It must have been his cunning and wits that somehow allowed him to avoid a horrible fate.

Working as a presser in a coat factory, Mr. Stossel may have been more comfortable performing that solitary occupation than mingling at a get-together in mixed company. He always seemed to be cautious about revealing too much of himself, and, therefore, he avoided lengthy conversations. I never even knew in which apartment he lived, having never been invited to it or followed him to it. However, he was distinct from the rest of the *grine* in a couple of ways.

He was a talented needle pointer, specializing in colorful pillows with raised stitches that featured swans and butterflies on a silk background. Each pillow was trimmed with bright red or blue velvet fabric. I wondered where he had learned this specialized craft, which many of the women sought and admired. Added to his skill as a renowned shofar blower on the High Holy Days, his array of talents certainly improved his prominence, despite his short stature, among the members of our community.

When one of our neighbors called him David instead of Jacob, his purported first name, I knew there was a lot more to Mr. Stossel than I may have thought. Also, when some of the *grine* referred to him as "the professor," I assumed he had either been a university professor at one time or he had at least attained a high level of education in his native land. He seemed to catch on to English more quickly than the rest of the group. I mused that perhaps he had already learned a little of the language in his home country, which happened to be the same as my mother's, Hungary. He and my mother's same native tongue, shared cultural experiences, and skill with a needle could have been the sources of a common ground for both of them.

But I never saw Mr. Stossel with any single ladies. His introverted personality made it difficult to know him. Once in a while, he and my mother would speak Hungarian together, and they both seemed relieved to converse in their native tongue. He even gave her one of his needlepoint masterpieces, a white swan fabrication, knowing that my mother, above all people, would understand the intense labor and design work required to complete it. But it never went any further. There was just too much mystery between the two of them.

One day in 1956, my mother had a special visitor. A woman she had met during her short time at Camp Wentorf, the transit camp where she had completed her visa documents before her departure for America, had come to visit from New York City. A shy, reserved Hungarian woman, she had formed a close friendship with my mother during that brief transition time. After losing her whole family during the war as well, Rozi kept in close touch with my mother after their arrival in the United States. She was a few years younger and perceived my mother as an older sister. It was heartwarming for me to see my mother as someone who meant so much as a mentor to a younger woman.

We brought Rozi to Ruby's Market during her stay with us to buy our week's groceries. As we stood in front of the breakfast cereal section in the small neighborhood grocery store, we bumped into Mr. Stossel. He looked up at us and noticed Rozi immediately.

Hello, Mr. Stossel, my mother said. *I vould like to introduce you to my good friend, Rozi Vinkler, fun New York. Ve know each oder fun Germany. She is a Hungarian too.*

Nagyon örülök hogy látom [very nice to meet you], Mr. Stossel said to Rozi in Hungarian, with a little gleam in his eye and keeping his neck stretched up so his eyes could meet hers. *I hope you are enjoying your visit.*

Yes, tank you. I am glad to be mit my friend, Sidi. It is very nice here in Springfield, Rozi said.

Vell, I am very glad to meet anoder Hungarian like Mrs. Perlstein. Dere are not too many of us here in Springfield, you know. Viszontlátásra. Goodbye. I hope I vill see you again before you leave. Maybe holnap [tomorrow]?

Mr. Stossel made a point of coming to our apartment for the first time the next day especially to see Rozi again. It must have been love at first sight. They seemed to have a lot in common as they were both shy, highly intelligent, and spoke the same language. They were married within the next month in New York, with my mother taking all the credit for their introduction. Soon after, Mr. Stossel moved to Brooklyn, New York, with his new bride. We visited them a number of times in the ensuing years, and I came to know Mr. Stossel more than I ever would have, had he remained in Springfield. I learned that, indeed, neither he nor his name were what they purported to be, but I am the last person ever to give his secrets away. I know how important secrets are to so many.

CHAPTER 31

The Games

We played hopscotch daily when the weather was nice on the city sidewalks in front of our block. Pieces of glass or stones found in the empty lot next door served as our markers, and blackboard chalk for the pavement or a stick for drawing the course in dirt served our needs.

Jumping rope was popular among the girls, either single or double Dutch. It was an easy and inexpensive pastime for us, as were all our games, and we spent many hours honing our timing and balance. Some of us became pretty proficient at jump rope but could never have competed against the best of today's jump rope prodigies.

Cat's cradle often occupied our time, especially when we were on a school bus or traveling in a car. It became one of our mainstay games until we were adolescents. All it required was a piece of tied string looped around each hand and then the positioning of our fingers in various ways to create new loops in different shapes and designs. The second player had to find ways to pick up the string from the previous player using only her fingers to create new shapes and configurations without letting go of the string. Cat's Eye and Diamonds were among our favorite looped designs.

Board games were also ubiquitous, especially checkers and Chinese checkers. By the time we were ten, though, we were obsessed with jacks, which tested our hand-eye coordination and reflexes.

Hanele, my mother shouted impatiently, *vhen are you and your friends finishing your jecks? Ve almost ready for supper.*

We are almost done, ma. I'm already up to ten, I replied. But it usually took quite some time to finish the games, and so my supper often had to wait.

For a while, I thought I would be playing with that small bouncing ball and those six-sided metal pieces for the rest of my life, since my friends and I could not resist playing no matter where we were. We carried around our little sacks with the pieces everywhere we went, always ready for a spontaneous game. However, as we grew older, during our last year or so on Osgood Street, and later in our new neighborhoods when we could get together, our games of choice invariably revolved around cards and sometimes dominoes.

Playing cards seemed like a natural progression from the earlier games of our youth. We had all seen the *grine,* with the notable exception of my mother, playing card games ever since we were very young, so it was not a stretch for us to take up Americanized versions of cards. The most popular game by far was Pitch, a variation of Setback, but played with eight cards instead of six. I cannot remember how that particular card game, featuring high, low, jack, and game as the basis of its points, had become the most frequent in our repertoire. I am fairly certain it was not a game played by the adult card players in our community. However, the desire to play Pitch after school and on weekends became a compulsion that consumed much of our free time.

However, it was the occasional game of dominoes that drew my mother's attention. I did not play the game often and never became a proficient player, yet the first time my mother saw me play, she stood and stared at the string of dominoes with an intense gaze. She looked at me, then over at the dominoes on the table, and then back at me as though she had a special understanding of the layout of the tiles and what should be my next move. In contrast to never taking notice of card playing, she seemed to have a strange interest in dominoes.

One evening at supper, soon after she had observed me playing the game, she told me a story about how a game of dominoes figured prominently at Dachau, one of the concentration camps she had experienced during the war. As one of twenty women on a work detail chosen to cook and clean at the nearby Schloss, a Bavarian castle near the camp, she walked every day in civilian clothing from the camp to the mansion. The aristocratic estate had been taken over by the German army, the Wehrmacht, which used it as its headquarters in the area. The soldiers often played table games, usually dominoes, during their off times.

> *Vell, you know my family in Hungary loved to play dominoes, and I knew how to play very good dominoes. I vas an expert.*
>
> *No kidding, ma. I never thought you liked games. But now I remember you once told me your family played dominoes at home.*
>
> *Ven I saw da soldiers playing dominoes, I look at von of der hent* [hands], *and stand over his shoulder. I vhisper to him about vhat he should do next. Does he have a domino he can play? I almost forgot vhere I vas. I couldn't help myself. Vhen da soldiers realize I am an expert player, dey keep me dere to give dem advice how to play. Each soldier vanted me to help him vin da game. So, every day, vhen I am at da cestle* [castle], *dey ask me to come over for a vhile to help mit da domino game.*
>
> *How did that make you feel, ma?* I asked her, making a rare emotional foray.
>
> *I feel a little bit like I am better den some of da soldiers. I know some tings dey don't know. But at da same time, I vas a prisoner, an I had to do vhat dey tell me.*

I never heard any more about this series of events. I sensed more occurred in this poignant Dachau tale, but I never asked again. As I grew older, I wondered whether the soldiers might have taken more advantage of my mother, the female prisoner who just happened to be a domino expert. Could it have been that her wartime experience with dominoes turned her away from ever playing games again?

CHAPTER 32

The Coin Collector

*H*ani, *dere is not enough coffee in my jar for my cup of coffee dis morning. I tink I have a new jar of Maxvell House on da shelf somevhere,* my mother announced as she started rising from her chair at our kitchen table.

Don't get up from the table, ma, I responded, standing up and putting my hand on her shoulder. *I'll find a fresh jar of your instant coffee. Just give me a minute.*

My mother usually never allowed me to do anything in the kitchen, except sometimes set the table or put our dirty dishes in the sink so she could wash them. She was the queen of our kitchen in every way. I was surprised when she said, *Tank you,* and sat back down in her seat.

When I walked over to the shelf in the kitchen where she kept her pantry supplies, I noticed for the first time that there were several jars of Maxwell House Instant Coffee. *I guess she likes to stock up on her favorite breakfast drink,* I said to myself. A small stovetop coffee percolator always stood on a burner of her stove, but she had never used it, preferring the ease of making instant coffee since she arrived in America.

However, as I picked up the first jar, I noticed that it was much heavier than the usual jar of instant coffee. Looking closer, I realized that it did not contain coffee at all, but was filled to the brim with pennies. A little puzzled, I put the jar back in its place and picked up the next one. To my amazement, this jar too contained coins, but this time, it was filled with nickels. I finally found a real jar of instant coffee and brought it out to the table.

> *Here it is ma. Now you can have your morning coffee,* I announced, putting the jar in front of her plate.
> *Oy, tank you, Hanele. I cen't start my morning mitout my coffee.*

Debating whether I should mention my coin discoveries to her, I decided not to do so, hoping that I would learn more about her collection on my own before asking her any questions. She must have forgotten about her Maxwell House coins or else she would not have agreed to allow me to fetch the jar. I resolved to explore her collecting habit a little further before bringing up the subject.

Once I had discovered the penny and nickel-filled jars, I decided to take a closer look at my mother's shelved food items. I was not used to spending too much time in the kitchen, except for eating, so I had never taken much notice of her canned and jarred food. I waited until one weekend when she was absorbed in one of her sewing projects, barely looking up from her sewing machine, and knew it was my golden opportunity.

I instantly noticed a couple of containers of Crisco shortening and took each one off of the shelf. Neither contained Crisco. One was filled with dimes and the other with quarters. A pickle jar behind one of the Crisco containers contained more quarters! I dared not open any of the containers to closely examine the coins inside, because it would take too much time and risk my mother's discovery. I dreaded her finding out about my sleuthing before I was ready to divulge it to her. Now that I knew about her coin collecting,

I wondered whether she had hidden any coins in other receptacles besides those in food containers.

My mother had taken to sewing cloth zippered bags in various sizes, which contained everything from makeup, bobby pins, sewing notions, to bank books, letters, and other papers, a trend she would continue for the rest of her life. No file folders for her. The bags were constructed from a range of fabrics, just like her clothing designs, such as cotton, faux leather, and suede. They came in an array of print and solid colors, many stitched over with her machine to resemble quilting material. I knew where she kept many of them.

Pretending that I was looking for my school photos, which I knew she had stored in one of her bureau drawers, I opened her bureau's bottom drawer. As I viewed a sea of her homemade zippered bags, I began to unzip two bags that lay underneath the school photos. The bigger one, measuring nine by eleven inches, contained about hundred coins, a mixture of quarters, half dollars, and silver dollars. The smaller one, measuring approximately nine by nine inches, contained an equally large assortment of nickels, dimes, and quarters. I knew then that my mother had probably been stocking away her coins for a very long time. I wanted to take a closer examination of the coins, but in order to accomplish that, I would have to tell my mother I had discovered them.

Ma, I noticed that some of your Maxwell House Coffee jars contain coins. How long have you been collecting?

Oy, you know me, Hanele, I'm alvays a saver. I love American money. I like da pictures on dem. Someday, ve vill roll dem up and take dem to da bank to deposit. I didn't vant to tell you until I vas ready to take dem to da bank.

She did not seem to mind that I had discovered her coin collection. If that was the case, I wondered why she had never told me about it before. I would have been willing to help her collect. Then again, she did not divulge so many things.

>   *Will you let me take a look at your coins up close?* I asked.
>   *Maybe there are some valuable ones that I can find.*
>   *Okay sure, if you vant to,* she acceded.

I spent the next few days using a magnifying glass to take a closer look at her coins, which I discovered in still more bags and containers. As a non-coin collector, however, I really did not know much about their value. However, I noticed that some of the dates on various coins were from long before the time I discovered them in 1957, with dates reaching as far back as 1928.

A few years later, we rolled the pennies, dimes, nickels and quarters and took them together to the bank for deposit in our small savings account. Not one coin was spared to convert to cash. However, the half dollars and silver dollars remained in their original containers, never rolled or deposited. They included the 1928 and 1934 Peace silver dollars launched in commemoration of the peace after World War I and the last dollar ever struck for circulation in real silver. These eventually were transferred a little at a time to her bank safe deposit box, where they remained until her death.

I never discussed my mother's coin collection with any of my friends. Like my mother, I thought it was just our business. However, one day about a year after my initial discovery, I was visiting the Landsmans.

>   *I see your mother and father also like Maxwell House Instant Coffee,* I noted to Yussie, observing some jars in their pantry.
>   *No, there's no coffee in them,* he replied. *Just coins.*

CHAPTER 33

The Freedom Fighters

It was hard not to notice the three Sklarz brothers. They were attractive, outgoing, good-natured, and almost happy-go-lucky in their outward manner. Three brothers who had survived the Holocaust and lived together in the same American city was a rare occurrence. That alone would have made them stand out in any small community.

They had married equally attractive women who seemed charmed by their husbands' confidence and cheer. I often saw them with Mr. and Mrs. Bart, a quiet, reserved couple whose personalities seemed in stark contrast to those of the Sklarz brothers. Yet, despite their personality differences, they all seemed to have a special kinship to one another, speaking effortless, fluent Yiddish.

My mother was an adequate Yiddish speaker, able to converse with relative ease with others among our community. As a Hungarian, however, she had not been raised speaking Yiddish as her primary language. Her family's daily conversation among each other and with the people of their village was Hungarian. When she spoke her native tongue, my mother was articulate. She enunciated every consonant and vowel emerging from her lips like a sculptor precisely shaping and smoothing her work of art. I marveled at how she positioned her mouth and tongue in ways not required or even possible by an English speaker. The Sklarzes and Barts, however, like most of the rest of the *grine*, were proficient Yiddish speakers, having spoken it as their primary language for most of their lives.

At a birthday party in honor of one of Leon Sklarz's daughters, I heard someone mention "Vilna." I thought I had heard one of the wives say, *Ikh ken Vilna nit fargesn* (I cannot forget Vilna). I wondered what or who Vilna could have been to her. It could have been the name of a lost family member, or a school they may have attended, or maybe it was a Polish or Lithuanian word for something else I could not interpret. My curiosity was piqued by the plaintive tone in which the woman had said "Vilna."

Ma, what is a Vilna? I asked my mother when we returned to our apartment.

Vhy you ask, Hanele? she replied, surprised by my question.

I just heard Mrs. Sklarz talk about it, and I wasn't sure what it was. Do you know?

Yes. It's a big town vhere da Litvaks come from, she responded. *Many Jews used to vonce live dere, and some of dem are here mit us in Springfield.*

Oh, I understand now, I said, realizing that the person mentioning the name of Vilna was wistfully remembering their former home.

So accustomed to hearing my mother's stories of Dámóc, her little village, where only five Jewish families lived among a small community of Greek Orthodox Catholics, I was astonished to hear about a large city in Europe containing many Jews. As I started to read a little about the history of the city called Vilna, I learned of the profound impact many generations of Jewish families had on the city referred to as the "Jerusalem of Lithuania," known for its rich Jewish cultural and academic centers. With the little information available in the 1950s about the Vilna Jews' terrible fate during World War II,

I could form only an inkling of what the Sklarz and Harts may have witnessed and experienced in their recent past.

The long-term suffering of Lithuanian Jews during World War II was emphasized during my summer trip to visit my cousins in Kansas City in 1959. My mother's first cousin Olga had married a Lithuanian survivor, Michael, who had his own success story in America as a renowned builder and construction innovator. Many years after his liberation, he could still barely control his anger at the Nazis for having subjected his family and Jewish compatriots to such a lengthy and traumatic ordeal, longer and more vicious than almost any other. My cousin's raw emotions so many years after the war revealed his terrible memories of events almost too dreadful to describe.

I did not learn of the enormous losses suffered by the Jews of Vilna until I was an adult. Nor was I cognizant, as a child, of the possible vital role the Sklarzes and the Barts played in resisting their oppressors. Once a bastion of Jewish culture, philosophy, and theology, Vilna's Jews constituted roughly forty percent of the city's population before World War II, with numbers ranging from 70,000 to possibly 100,000 residents. During the early part of the war, starting in 1939, the country's rule shifted from Poland to Russia to Lithuania, and finally in 1941, to the new Soviet Union.

By the fall of 1941, however, with Nazi Germany's invasion of Lithuania in the preceding summer, the Jews of Vilna and those in other Lithuanian cities had been herded into ghettos. There they lived under distinctly inhumane conditions of malnutrition, humiliation, submission, and ever-increasing losses due to deportations to concentration camps or murder. Although they had, over the centuries, experienced the overt anti-Semitism of their Lithuanian and Polish neighbors, the brutality and sheer breadth of the Nazi operation in their city and country was enormous by comparison.

Unlike the Jews of my mother's homeland, whose experience I had learned through her stories, the Lithuanian Jews were not lulled into thinking they would be spared the death and destruction of the Holocaust. They were not as naive as some of the Jews in the Hungarian countryside, who acknowledged the anti-Jewish laws enacted by their Regent, Miklos Horthy, yet also mistakenly believed their country was adequately civilized to avoid what was occurring in the rest of Europe. In contrast, occupied by Nazi forces early in World War II, the Lithuanian Jews were among the first forced into ghettos and killing fields immediately upon the entrance of the German army into their land — three years before Eichmann and his Kommando had set up their operation in Hungary.

Two ghettos were originally established in Vilna. A small one, containing the elderly and others judged unfit for work, was quickly liquidated, meaning that all its inhabitants were killed. Because the residents were shot mainly at the open pits of the nearby Ponary Forest — a once-carefree location for leisurely family outings —the Jews viewed the pits of Ponary over the next two years as a fate synonymous with instant death.

The second and larger ghetto remained in existence until 1943, when all its inhabitants were liquidated through the ghetto's inhumane conditions, death marches, and extermination at Ponary, deportation to concentration camps, and other spontaneous killings by Nazi forces and their Lithuanian police collaborators. The term *liquidation* was used as though the extermination of live human beings was akin to the bankruptcy of an economic enterprise or the dissolution of some other inanimate asset.

In fact, while I was studying the history of Lithuanian Jews or any of the other elements of the human torture inflicted during the Holocaust, I was always confronted by such innocuous words as *liquidation, final solution, relocation,* and *selection.* These words were strangely the same as those used in a bank ledger or financial document. The inhumanity of it all called up a picture of suffering so demanding to the heart and brain that those who had not lived it could not grasp it. Moreover, those who had perpetrated it insisted on hiding its savagery by using such euphemisms.

Amid the chaos of the Vilna ghetto, the Jewish freedom fighters emerged. A small band of men and women had taken on the role of disrupting the Nazi war machine by creating an underground unit within the ghetto. Their motto, "We shall not be led like sheep to slaughter," was a rallying slogan dating back to the words of George Washington speaking to his army officers. Almost two millennia before Washington, the Jewish martyrs, during the Roman destruction of the second temple, realized that the time of armed resistance was no longer an option and submitted to their deaths free of despair and horror, giving in to divine decree. In the case of the Vilna freedom fighters, their position included armed resistance, defiance to the end, and dying with dignity if they could not survive.

Eventually, by the fall of 1943, faced with the certain prospect of the total annihilation of those left within the ghetto, the freedom fighters found their way through the stinking, slimy sewers under the streets of Vilna to the nearby forests to join the partisans, who were bent on destroying the flow of German soldiers and supplies. They could no longer save their fellow prisoners inside the ghetto, yet they risked their lives to thwart a Nazi victory and hasten the war's end.

Using stolen rifles, machine guns, revolvers, and explosives, they succeeded in blowing up trains and severing water and infrastructure resources while also acting in their own defense in the often treacherous forest against nearby farmers and Lithuanian or Russian partisans who had no use for Jewish freedom fighters. The "liquidation" of the ghetto was as swift and vicious as they had anticipated, with only a few hundred survivors, mainly those attached to a small labor camp whose benevolent commandant managed to save some of his workers from the SS. The Jerusalem of Lithuania, admired for centuries, had come to a reprehensible end.

At one time, I wondered whether the Sklarz brothers and the Barts could have been part of the resistance movement in their homeland. The spirited brothers seemed to exhibit the kind of behavior that made that idea plausible. They could have acted as renegades and defied authority in the previous decade. Since few survivors of Vilna existed, they could easily have been involved with the partisans, I thought. However, the Barts were so quiet and unassuming that I did not think they had the energy or motivation to take on the risks required of a stealth operation. They barely raised their voices.

These days, I understand how the appearances of the *grine* were not even close to being a true reflection of their complete character. Perhaps the Sklarz brothers were, indeed, members of the Jewish partisans, or maybe not. By chance, I just recently came across the story of a couple that had fallen in love in Vilna and had ventured into the dangers of heroism together to foil a Nazi victory. Their son had written an account of his parents' bravery and sacrifices in *Until Our Last Breath: A Holocaust Story of Love and Partisan Resistance.*

Contrary to my childhood observations, it was both Mr. and Mrs. Bart who were members of the Vilna underground and partisans in the forest, learning how to deploy arms, strike at the enemy, and risk their lives to fight another day. In America, they took on their new personae, putting their daring adventures behind them and quietly slipping into American society without ever betraying their brutal past. Their courage, as with so many of the *grine*, was beyond formidable.

CHAPTER 34

The Ring

My mother never owned any real jewelry during all the years she lived in America. Many of the women in our community wore the expensive jewels their husbands had purchased for them once they had established themselves in their new country. The husbands did not want to deprive their wives of some of the luxury items desired by most American women. My mother, however, spent her money mainly on food and rent, other necessities, and sewing notions. Since she wore no makeup except lipstick, she attempted to dress up her looks occasionally with a piece of inexpensive costume jewelry.

The rhinestone bow pin

An imitation gold comb-and-brush set, purchased at Forbes and Wallace soon after her coming to America, lay on a white doily on the surface of her bureau, never moved or even touched. The top drawer contained the many jewelry items she had collected beginning with our time on Osgood Street, which were usually stored in their original boxes. When I looked into her drawer, I often pretended that all the pieces were real gold and diamonds. They included a rhinestone bow pin, a cloudburst rhinestone brooch, brass-swirl clip-on earrings, an imitation pearl necklace, a Mexican hatpin, and imitation pearl-drop clip-on earrings. No real gold, diamond, or even gemstone jewelry ever made it into her collection, with one exception.

Among her imitation jewelry lay the only ring in her drawer — a thick, majestic-looking, all-gold ring. Much heavier than the rest of her jewelry, it showcased a raised rectangular face that was a little scuffed, as though something had once been pasted onto its surface. The soft gold band was bent to one side, likely having been dropped at one time and never repaired. Although it was obviously some sort of signet ring, I always imagined that it was a ring my father had given to my mother, perhaps as a substitute wedding ring. Adding to the ring's mystique, my mother never wore it, at least not in my presence.

I asked her about it only one time, when I was eight years old.

Ma, this ring looks different. Where did you get it? I asked when I was standing beside her as she opened her bureau drawer to reach for one of her rhinestone pins.

Oy, dat's noting. It's just a ring fun Germany. Vonce, it had my initials, PS, for Perlstein Sidonia, on it, but it fall off. Now I just keep et in my bureau.

I never asked her again about the ring I had noticed in her drawer, and she never spoke of it. It lay there, the only unboxed piece, until she died. And it lay in my bedroom bureau drawer, still untouched and unrepaired after her death, for a long time. I never quite believed my mother's explanation about the ring. I was sure its source was something different from her account.

Besides not having had money to buy jewelry or a partner to buy any for her, I wondered whether the reason my mother had not purchased any genuine jewels was that she had left the real ones at home in Hungary. After hearing her stories about the hidden jewelry her family had placed in a metal box behind a brick in their kitchen hearth before their abrupt departure, I reasoned that she had not had the heart to replace those family heirlooms. Any new genuine jewelry purchased in America would have been poor replicas and reminders of the precious items that had belonged to her mother, father, and siblings.

Later, when I turned sixteen and graduated from high school, my mother surprised me with a beautiful gold-chain charm bracelet. Its first charm hung from one of the delicate chains. It was the number sixteen inside a brushed gold circle adorned with four small gemstones. The engraved inscription read, *Happy Sixteenth Birthday, Love, Mother.* She had saved buying any genuine jewels in America until she had a special occasion to buy them for me.

After my mother passed, I brought her gold signet ring to a jeweler for buffing and repair. I could not bear to allow it to rest in my drawer any longer, lest it somehow lose its fascination or perhaps be forgotten, never to be worn again. As I lay the piece on the counter, the jeweler picked it up to look through her magnifier to evaluate the gold and check for any inscription or other markings. As she did this, she spoke:

> *I thought you'd like to know. At one time, a "P" and an "S" were glued to the face of this ring.*
> *Does that mean anything to you?* she asked.
> *Yes,* I replied. *Those were the initials of the original owner.*

My mother's story about the ring was true. It had once borne her initials, "P" and "S," last name first. But how and where she obtained it remained her secret.

The signet ring, buffed and repaired

CHAPTER 35

The Farm

The stench was pervasive on that summer Sunday morning. It hit me as soon as I stepped out of the car. Tightly squeezing my nostrils together with my fingers to avoid the stink, I did not think I could stay too long at the chicken farm. *This is not the place for me,* I thought to myself. *How can they stand it here?* My city girl nose was almost disjointed by the pungent odors of raw nature.

But my mother urged me to say hello to the Landsmans and thank them for having invited us to their farm. I covered my nose with my fist and walked up to the front door of the white clapboard farmhouse, where Mrs. Landsman was waiting for us.

Hi, Mrs. Landsman, I said, taking my fist away from my nose, but trying not to inhale. *Thank you for inviting us to see your chickens.*

I made my cake just for you, Chanele, Mrs. Landsman replied, *because you didn't have a chance to taste it last time. Ve also have fresh eggs to eat and for you to take home.*

Oh, great. Thank you. The mention of the mocha cake evoked the memory of the most beautiful, sweet aroma that had ever swirled through my nostrils and supplanted the acrid odor, at least for a while.

Mr. Landsman and Yussie led me to the chicken coops, where the chickens were roaming, pecking, and scratching. As I gazed at the chickens surrounded by a netting of chicken wire, I noticed their heads were bobbing back and forth as though attempting to dislodge something from their throats. The clucking bird noises and busy activity reminded me of the pigeons that inhabited the eaves of the house next to my bedroom, helping to settle my nervousness. At the same time, I observed that my mother had strategically slipped inside the house, apparently not too interested in visiting the chickens.

I watched as Mr. Landsman and Yussie changed the bucket of water and refilled the feeder with replenished chicken feed inside one of the coops. I certainly did not want to help with any of those tasks myself. Although my nose had become accustomed to the smell, no longer bothered by the stinging bite of chicken fragrance, I could not wait to leave the farm. *Let me just have a piece of that cake, and I'll be glad to leave,* I said to myself.

But then, just as I was turning to head over to the farmhouse, Mr. Landsman asked, *How vould you like to take some eggs into da house, Chanele? Our hens are laying eggs for us every day. See if you can find some eggs vhere da hens are sitting in dere boxes, and put dem in dis basket.*

Taking the basket from his hand, I looked at the birds in their nesting boxes and reached into one of the nests, retrieving a light brown, speckled egg and laying it in the basket. Walking down the row of hens, I reached into several more nests and pulled out an egg each time.

When my basket was filled with a dozen eggs, Mr. Landsman said, *Go show your moder vhat you pick from da hen house. She vill be surprised.*

Exhilarated by having plucked eggs from the nesting boxes, I ran back to the farmhouse with my basket, my mouth burst wide in a rare glowing smile. *Look what I found ma,* I said in my excitement. *Mr. Landsman said we could keep the eggs to bring home. Did you ever see anything like it, ma?*

A long time ago, Hanele. Yeh, a long time ago, my mother replied with a chuckle, remembering the chickens that had roamed her backyard in Hungary.

We ate scrambled eggs and mocha cream cake before we left to return to Osgood Street, carrying our carton of speckled eggs with us. The memory of my visit to the pastoral setting of the chicken farm stayed with me for a long time. Despite the thrill of finding the fresh eggs, though, I had grown accustomed to my urban upbringing and never desired to visit the farm again.

In contrast, the Landsmans had found the kind of peaceful life in an agricultural setting that made them content. They tried to make a go of it, selling eggs to wholesalers and the public and enjoying the wonders of grassy meadows, trees, wildflowers, and nearby streams for wading and fishing. Those marvels of existence were impossible to find in the city. Yet, despite their hard work, the Landsmans found themselves back in the city before long, seeking a predictable paycheck, a cycle they would encounter several more times before their final abandonment of farming.

CHAPTER 36

Reinvention

The *grine* were as adept as professional actors at making the world seem like something it was not. They were like spies who were pretending to be quiet, modest, average American citizens involved with the mundane responsibilities of life, yet also contending with the lives they had invented by necessity in the wake of their Holocaust experiences.

During their early years in Springfield, many Americans, Jews and non-Jews, encouraged them to forget their wartime experiences and to forge new lives. Although the concept of creating new lives was admirable, at the same time, it was unrealistic and psychologically detrimental to encourage them to forget the horrors of their recent past. The good intentions of Americans inadvertently created a culture of secrets and served instead to impel the *grine* to hide their victimization from everyone around them in order to be accepted in their adopted land.

Is that an accent I detect? So where are you from? asked the supervisor during an interview at one of the dress factories before my mother was hired at the Victoria Dress Corporation.

I am from Hungary.

So what brings you to America? How long have you been here?

Vell, I have been here about two years. I vas in concen-tration camps during da var an I couldn't go back home, my mother replied not too long after our arrival.

Oh, well, I'm so sorry. We don't want to talk about that, do we? Let's see how you do at one of our sewing machines, okay?

I suspect that all the other members of our immigrant community experienced similar encounters, causing them to band together even more cohesively and to keep a tight lid on their secrets.

Age deception, for example, was common. When I accompanied Mrs. Stern to the motor vehicle department to obtain her driver's license, I saw her take her citizenship papers from her purse before handing them to the official as proof of birth. As I quickly gazed over at the documents before she placed them on the counter, I thought 1920 was written as the year of her birth, which would have made her thirty-five years old at the time. Yet only the week before, I had heard her say to her husband:

Listen, Shloyme, don't eat dat cake. You know it don't agree vit you. I'm older den you, I know.

Oy, Lenya, leave me alone, responded her husband in an irritated voice. *You are only von year older, 1915, 1916, who cares?*

After witnessing these two episodes, I did not know what to believe. When and why had Mrs. Stern changed her age? What could have been the reason for the different birth dates? Through the years of my time on Osgood Street, I observed similar circumstances among the rest of the *grine*. Most of them seemed to have lied about their ages, either before, during, or after the war, to gain an advantage in some way.

Even some of the other residents of our building, who were not members of our immigrant community, seemed to lie about their ages. The divorced woman who brought me a piece of her blueberry pie from across the back porch told us she was forty-five. She had been laid off from her job as a waitress and was desperate for some income to pay her next month's rent.

My mother was in the process of relighting the pilot light at the rear of her gas oven, which had unexpectedly gone out, when our neighbor burst through our back door, which was often open during the day when we were home. As usual, she seemed to be in a hurry to tell us her latest piece of juicy gossip, her dish of pie in one hand.

Hey, Sonia [a mispronunciation of my mother's name], *guess what? The restaurant let me go. Not enough business.*

Vhat you gonna do now, Nancy? my mother asked, backing away from the oven and blowing out the match.

I'm gonna have to find a new job, but at my age, it's hard. I'm gonna have to tell 'em I'm thirty-six when I go for the job interviews, she told us. *Makes me more employable, don't ya think?*

Believe me, I know vhat you mean, my mother said in a sympathetic tone.

Ya know, if I told 'em my real age, I don't think I'd ever find a job, Nancy added.

Not until I was well into adulthood did I realize that my mother was among those who had lied about her age even before she entered the United States. Fearing her thick legs, with their increasing varicosity, would earmark her for death in a concentration camp, she had begun to lie about her age, making herself younger to offset this detrimental feature and save her life. She continued to lie after the war until she eventually adjusted her age downward by six years. All her American documents, including her driver's license, medical records, and citizenship papers, displayed her fabricated birth year.

I think she almost believed the invalid birth date herself until she became sixty-two and was eligible for her Social Security benefits. Then, an inner voice must have shaken and prodded her to remember her accurate age. At one time, it may have been to her advantage to pretend to be younger, but then it became the reverse. It was more advantageous to be older in order to provide her with an adequate living income.

After securing her Hungarian birth certificate, she was able to show her real birth date to the Social Security office. She had entered the country at the age of thirty-six instead of thirty, as I had always thought, but she had hidden it so well, I was thunderstruck when the birth document revealed her true age. I felt deceived and disappointed that she had not shared this important piece of information with me. If she were six years older, would I lose her sooner than I had anticipated? I found it difficult to wrap my head around this new information.

One member of the *grine*, Mrs. Bach, offered a twist to the age deception. She had the uncanny ability to remember everyone's birth date, whether the date was legitimate or not. A vast array of dates and numbers appeared stored in her brain. If she heard an adult or child's birth date, she could recall it months and even years later.

When one of us children tried to trick her by telling her a different date than the one she had memorized, she retorted, *Ach, now you're trying to trick me, but I know da trut [truth]. You can't fool me.*

Many years later, when I saw her at a wedding, she recognized me and tossed out my birth date as though she had learned it only the day before.

It's you, Hanele. August 29, right? she asked, and added, *Your moder gave up her life for you. She vas something.*

I wondered whether Mrs. Bach's ability to remember a mountain of dates also coincided with recalling all the emotions attached to many of them. If so, the burden must have been excruciating. However, Mrs. Bach's innate skill allowed her to act as the repository of information about each and every person in our community.

More lies related to first and last names, sometimes totally changed and at other times just tweaked. I was never sure whether anyone among the *grine* were telling the truth about his or her name. Mr. Stossel's real name, as it turned out, was totally different from the one he used in America, but he continued to use the fake one all his life, too afraid to reveal his deception of many years earlier to gain entrance to the United States. Lottie Burman, for example, who sometimes took care of me when Mrs. Kester was unavailable, was always referred to by the name of Bela. What could have been the reason for her name change? Whom to believe?

Another area where many of the members of my neighborhood kept secrets related to the former spouses and children they had in their native lands before the war. Many of them appeared to be in their thirties, which meant it was conceivable for them to have been married and given birth to children in the past. Sometimes they were able to share facts about their lost families with their children, but often they could not summon the psychological strength to convey the details. Often they felt the need to shield their children from their past for fear that it would crush their happiness and diminish their self-confidence. Now, as an adult, I cannot imagine how much those thoughts must have generated tremendous traumatic strain for so many of the individuals with whom I grew up.

Their wartime experiences as fighting partisans, hidden prey, concentration camp victims, or people with assumed identities were well hidden by the time they reached Osgood Street. All I could detect was the undercurrent of suspicious circumstances. As a child, it was not difficult for me to love them.

As for my mother, I knew that she had withheld important facts from me for as long as I can remember. Like most of the *grine*, my mother had carefully selected stories to reveal to a child whom she wished to protect from what she believed to have been the most disgraceful and shameful events of her former life. Although I desperately wanted to know much more, especially about my father, I had also developed her pattern of secrecy and restraint. The dichotomous forces of intense love and general distrust continued to permeate our relationship. Yet, all the while, down deep, I understood that she was my one true partner, someone who loved me unconditionally, without any boundaries or limitations.

CHAPTER 37

The Matchmaker: A Revelation and a Warning, Progress Report 5

I never lost sight of my goal of obtaining a husband for my mother. I knew Mr. Olchinski's whereabouts most of the time when he was not working at Springfield Hospital as a maintenance worker. With movie-star good looks, an outgoing, amiable personality, and a dry sense of humor, he was popular with everyone, especially all the women. It was not only I who observed him with intense admiration. One might have called him the Polish-Jewish Cary Grant.

I had been trying to find my way into his good graces for several years without any success in coaxing him to get to know my mother. Not that she seemed to care. If he was standing alone at any time in my presence, I stored my innate shyness away and approached him to ask a question about his job at the hospital or whether he liked Ike, our country's president, or what he ate most often at Klibanoff's Delicatessen. My litany of questions seemed endless when it came to Mr. Olchinski. I think I came off sounding a little desperate after a while because one time, in the mid-1950s, he asked, *Hanele, do you have any friends you like to play vit? Maybe you should be vit dem.*

Yes, I do have lots of friends. I happen to be waiting for one of them right now. We're going to walk down Main Street over to the Jefferson Theatre to see a kids' double feature today. You know it's only a quarter, I spouted, even though I was not waiting for a friend at all. It was obvious I was making him nervous, so I had to be careful not to appear to be stalking him. It was hard.

Vell, have a good time den, he remarked, patting me on the shoulder as though prodding me to move on from his presence.

The Jefferson Theatre, 1973, courtesy of the Springfield (Massachusetts) History Library and Archives

Meanwhile, I saw Mr. Goodman and his wife come back to our apartment building a few times to see their friends among the *grine* and to play cards, bringing their new baby girl with them. I had given up trying to smile at him as I knew he would only turn his head aside, as usual.

Yussie, I asked my friend, *have you noticed that Mr. Goodman doesn't seem to like me very much?*

Nah, I don't think it has anything to do with not liking you, Yussie replied. *He just has some hard feelings.*

About what? I asked.

I don't know. I'm really not sure. I just think I heard that Mrs. Zagruder tried to fix him up with your mother a while ago and it didn't work out.

No, I retorted with an incredulous look on my face. *That can't be true. I think I would have known about that, wouldn't I?*

There are a lot of things you don't know, Hanna. Just add that to the collection.

If what Yussie told me was true, it helped me to put into perspective the contemptible looks my mother and I had always received from him. Although I will never know the details of what occurred between my mother and Mr. Goodman, it was plain his pride was wounded by their interaction. She could have spurned his attention in a manner that he perceived as offensive. It was apparent that he did not wish to face her, and by extension, me, again.

Judging by my mother's seemingly flippant attitude toward him, she may have felt the same. Perhaps she wanted to reciprocate his interest, but something inside her did not allow it. Learning the detail that Yussie had revealed to me, I realized my mother's dismissive posture was just a cover for her true feelings about a man who had made an overture to her, but it also evoked her sense of disappointment and even cynicism regarding her past relationships with men. Two prideful people, my mother and Mr. Goodman, had ended up in a standoff regarding their real emotions. If only pride had let down its guard, who knows what may have occurred between the two of them?

A strange thing happened after my brief conversation with Mr. Olchinski. Adina had decided to join me in walking to the Jefferson Theatre when I saw Mr. Rosenlicht standing nearby with his oldest son, Simmy, a chubby, taciturn, peculiar boy, apt to wear a black wool cap atop his head and avoid eye contact. Mr. Rosenlicht waved his hand at me as though summoning me to come toward him. Not sure what I should do, having no idea why he would want to see me, I hesitated for a few seconds. But my curiosity instinctively nudged me to turn to Adina and say, *Please wait for me. I'm just gonna go over to talk with Mr. Rosenlicht. I'll be back in a minute.*

When Mr. Rosenlicht saw me walking toward him, he motioned to his son to excuse him, and he moved a few feet away, so his son could not hear the ensuing conversation. As I arrived and stood close to him, his rather tall, lean form bent over, and he said:

Hanele, maybe it's not my business, but I don't vant you to be hurt, he whispered.

What do you mean?

Vatch out for Mr. Olchinski. I see you sometime looking at him. He is not a serious guy. I don't know vhat you vant, but he is not da right guy.

Uh, I really don't want anything from him, I retorted, hoping my lie did not seem too obvious.

Okay, okay. It's your business. I just vanted to tell you vhat is on my mind. I hope you vill tink about it. Zay gezint [be healthy, goodbye].

Thanks, I will. I said. *Goodbye.*

I turned to walk back toward Adina, who had a quizzical look on her face as she waited for my return.

What was that all about? she asked.

Nothing really, I responded. *Not worth talking about. All I want now is some popcorn.*

As we walked to the theater, I tried to make sense of Mr. Rosenlicht's warning. *What was he talking about? Why was Mr. Olchinski not the "right guy?"* I had never spoken directly to Mr. Rosenlicht before. *Who was he to tell me what to do?* I placed the warning squarely in the back of my head. I knew what I wanted despite what Mr. Rosenlicht thought. So I did not pay too much heed to his avuncular words.

CHAPTER 38

The Forever Kind of Gratitude

Vould you like to come vit me to da post office, Chanele? asked Mrs. Lott.

Okay, I'll ask my mother.

Since Lena Lott was one of my mother's best friends, it was easy to obtain my mother's permission to take the walk to the post office with her. We walked south on Dwight Street toward the nearest branch location. She carried a rather large, neatly taped box in both her hands.

Can I hold one end of the box and help you carry it? I guess it would have been easier if we had a ride to the post office.

Yes, you can take da oder end, and ve can valk slowly. It's not dat far. I couldn't find anyvon today who could give me a ride, and I didn't vant to vait any longer to send dis package. So here ve are taking a valk.

It's all right by me. I like to walk in the springtime, and besides, this box isn't that heavy.

As I carried one end of the box, I noticed it was addressed to a name I could not even come close to pronouncing. Its destination was a city or town in Poland. The contents of the box did not make any sound or slide around inside, so I guessed either it was very tightly packed or whatever was in there was not the kind of item that could be easily jostled. Even though I was curious, I decided not to ask Mrs. Lott about the intended recipients of the package or what was inside, at least not then.

After a longer walk than I had anticipated, we finally made it to the post office, where Mrs. Lott laid the container on the floor as soon as we got inside the door. Luckily, no one else was standing in line.

> *I vould like to send dis box to Poland, please,* Mrs. Lott said while walking up toward the man behind the counter.
>
> *Yes, ma'am. Let me pick it up for you and take it around the counter to weigh it. Then I'll help you fill out the customs form.*
>
> *Tank you. I have done dis a few times before so I understand vhat you need,* she said with a firm voice.
>
> *I thought I recognized you. You were just here last month,* said the postal worker. *What kind of material is inside?*
>
> *Just clothes,* she replied.

After filling out the proper paperwork, obtaining all the official postal labels, and paying for the postage, we said goodbye and left to return to our apartment building.

With no box to carry, it was a much faster walk home, a good time for conversation and an opportunity to satisfy my curiosity. I decided to ask some questions about the mysterious package we had just mailed to Poland.

> *Mrs. Lott, do you mind if I ask who is going to receive the box we just mailed?*
>
> *No, I don't mind. A family in Poland vill receive da box. It's clothes for der children. Ve try to send dem something vhen ve can.*

Who are they? I asked.

It's hard to explain, but if it vasn't for dis family, I vould not be alive today.

Wow, they sound like very important people.

Yes, dey are very important to us. Dey vere farmers near vhere ve lived in Poland. During da var, dey hide us underneat der barn for a very long time. After da var, ve told dem ve vould never forget dem. Never.

It's really nice of you to still be thinking about them. How long do you think you will keep sending them these packages?

Oh, forever.

I was silent on the rest of the way home.

Illegal Inventory

The details were kept hush-hush. I never heard anyone in my community overtly talk about it. If it were not for my mother bringing it up nonchalantly, I might never have known about it at all. Maybe it was my community's tendency to cover up any *shandes* (shameful events) in their past or present that allowed the episode to remain a secret.

As a group, the *grine* worked hard at jobs requiring tough physical labor in the first few years after their arrival in America. They were willing to take any kind of work in order to support their families. Resourceful and energetic, most of the men and women sought employment in the manufacturing and industrial sectors of a still economically vibrant city. Some of them obtained jobs in the health care industry as cooks, laboratory workers, or maintenance staff.

Yet, even though they lived in a low-rent neighborhood, it was often difficult to make ends meet. Sometimes it required each of them to take on two or more jobs to supply all life's necessities. Unfortunately, in one case, a couple with two children felt they had no other option but to secretly pinch items, a little at a time, from one of their employers to help support their family, convincing themselves it was for the greater good.

Mr. and Mrs. Bialychek were popular among the *grine*. They were devoted members of the card-playing crowd, often hosting a game at their apartment. They were generous with their home, time, and support for those in need. I liked that about them. Their goal was to purchase a home goods business, specializing in kitchen supplies, home decor, and tools for home repair and maintenance. Together, they offered considerable skill and expertise as kitchen and maintenance workers.

My mother was at her ironing board one day, gently flattening a wool skirt's side seam with her hot steam iron, when she turned to me and asked, *So da Bialycheks vill have to stay qviet for a while, don't you tink?*

> *I don't know, ma. Why?*
>
> *Vell, I tink dat vhen dey cetch you taking someting dat don't belong to you, dey vant to punish you? No?*
>
> *What are you talking about, ma?* I asked, assuming that "dey" referred to people in authority.
>
> *Da Bialycheks took cens* [cans] *of food and kitchen tings from da hospital for a long time. Dey really needed et, you know. But it vasn't right.*
>
> *Oh, ma. They must have been really desperate.*

Working at not much higher than minimum wage for a number of years, the Bialycheks had found it impossible to meet their everyday expenses. Little by little, through Mrs. Bialychek's job in the hospital kitchen, they had removed small amounts of canned food and kitchen supplies, hoping no one in authority would notice the missing items. One day, however, the manager in charge caught them in the act. Mrs. Bialychek was fired immediately, and both she and Mr. Bialychek were warned never to set foot on the premises again. At the same time, everyone at the hospital recognized their dire financial straits, so they decided not to press charges against them. Besides, up to then, Mrs. Bialychek was the best kitchen employee they had ever had.

The *grine*'s reaction was less conflicted than mine, or perhaps they just did not show it. Outwardly, instead of recrimination and scorn, as might have occurred in some other communities, they seemed to feel only empathy for the Bialycheks. The couple had tried their best to succeed in America but had temporarily failed. The community rallied around to support them. Some of them may have revisited the harsh, hidden acts they had been forced to undertake during the war in order to survive. Maybe it was all a matter of survival when faced with unfairness and injustice. However, the Bialycheck's dream of owning a home goods store never came true.

Part Four: Maturation

CHAPTER 40

The Facts of Life

She was a very pretty girl. At fourteen, she looked much more mature than her chronological age. Confidence flowed out of her every pore, giving the impression that she was proud of her looks and her budding physique. Wearing flawless face makeup and sporting long, wavy, brown hair, she was in a league of her own among the children of the *grine*.

Pearl and I both attended the Springfield Hebrew Institute after school three days a week. I usually walked home with some of my classmates after school to our Osgood Street apartments. On one occasion, however, when I had stayed a little later than usual, I found myself walking side by side with Pearl. Since she was more than three years my senior, I was not sure whether we had enough in common to converse easily with each other, and besides, I was a bit intimidated by her presence.

After crossing the street from our Hebrew school, we both automatically entered the tiny corner candy store, teeming with candies from bubble gum to jawbreakers. Purchasing some multicolored candy buttons on paper tape for a nickel, we each bit the candy dots off the paper and sucked on the sweet confections all the way home. As we walked, our conversation started out innocently enough about our respective Hebrew teachers and what we liked and did not like about their teaching styles.

I feel so bad for Mr. Zagorin when the class takes advantage of him. Maybe he's just too old to be teaching anymore, I said.

He probably likes teaching too much to stop, Pearl replied. *He's just a dedicated guy, I guess. I have Mr. Moses, you know, and he's probably just as old, but he's pretty feisty. He knows how to keep our class in shape, that's for sure,* she chuckled.

Yeah, I'm sure you're right.

Then, changing the subject, she mused, *I almost didn't come to Hebrew School today, because I had cramps this morning. It's my time of the month, and all I wanted to do was go home right after school and lie down.*

Gee, sorry you're not feeling well. This happens to you every month?

Yeah, you know, when it's my time.

Your time for what?

Uh, you know, my time to have my period.

You're gonna have to explain what you're talking about, I said, in a highly quizzical tone. *'Cause I have no idea.*

You mean you don't know anything about that time of the month?

No, can you tell me? I asked impatiently.

Sure, I can tell you, she retorted with no hesitation. *Every month, a woman bleeds down there for a few days. It has something to do with that place in your body where babies develop. It sheds its lining, and it comes out as blood. You have to wear a sanitary pad so you don't bleed on your clothes. You should start having it pretty soon.*

My head was spinning as though I were in orbit around a world that had drastically changed in a matter of minutes when Pearl told me of a woman's fate. That feeling of being in a world that was radically different from the one I knew would only happen to me a few times more in my life. Unlike my mother and the rest of the *grine*, I had grown up in a world that was totally familiar. I had never been transported against my will to places where strange and evil forces enveloped me. At almost eleven years old, I was entirely parochial in my view of the universe. My existence had been utterly predictable until my walk with Pearl. I stopped sucking on my candy dots, feeling sick to my stomach.

Are you sure about this, Pearl? Really sure? I questioned, hoping her story was just a concoction to play with a younger girl's mind. *I've never heard anything like it before. No one before you has ever told me about it.*

Even before her reply, I was already thinking that this was yet another secret my mother had neglected to share with me. How many more secrets existed? Would there be new revelations that would also turn my world upside down?

> *Yes, I'm absolutely sure,* she said. *I have it myself, so I know firsthand that it's true. You get used to it after a while. It's not so bad. Is that all you want to know?*
>
> *I think that's enough for me right now. If there's more, I don't want to hear about it,* I told her.

If I had said yes to her question about whether I wanted to know more, she may very well have clued me in on how babies were conceived, but I could not have handled it. I was in the dark about that until my pediatrician, Dr. Newmark, guessing my mother would never share the necessary details, prescribed a paperback book about female anatomy, the maturation of a girl's body, and the role of the reproductive organs. After reading it many times from cover to cover to digest all its contents and to confirm Pearl's narration and much more, I wondered whether Dr. Newmark had prescribed the same book to my other friends, whose parents were also unable to share the facts of life with them. It was funny that no one other than Pearl had ever mentioned the subject of menstruation.

Meanwhile, back on that day when Pearl and I discussed my impending maturation, we had finally finished our short walk from Chestnut Street, down Brookline Avenue to Dwight Street and then turned onto Osgood Street. We said our goodbyes and each headed for our respective apartments without my ever mentioning our discussion or thanking her for the bombshell news. When I entered our apartment, my mother was already home from work. *Vhat happen today, Hanele? Anyting new?* she asked.

No, not really, ma, I responded. *Just the same old stuff.*

CHAPTER 41

The Last Bachelor

By the end of the 1950s, the only remaining bachelor among the *grine* was the one I had my heart set on all along. Mr. Olchinski fit my dream of a father figure better than anyone else. After several years of following him, I finally came up with a plan to get him and my mother together at last. I knew he loved to play cards with the card-playing group. I often saw him sitting at a table gazing intently at his hand of cards with his legs crossed, a cigarette in his mouth, and a bottle of Knickerbocker beer in front of him. He still looked as captivating as any man had ever looked to me.

One autumn Sunday afternoon, as our New England maple trees began to shed their glistening bronze- and orange-hued leaves on the sidewalks outside our block, I waited for Mr. Olchinski on the back stairs. I knew he would soon be leaving his card game to go back to his apartment, and I wanted an opportunity to talk to him alone. When I spotted him, I was surprised at my own boldness in swiftly approaching him.

Oh, oh, hi, Mr. Olchinski. I was hoping to see you. I know you play cards a lot and I was wondering if you could teach me one of the card games you always play. My friends and I love to play cards, and your game looks, uh, very interesting, I sputtered without taking a breath.

Okay, Hanele, if you vant. Maybe I can come to your

apartment next week. I vill bring da deck of cards I use to play and teach you von of our Polish games. Make sure your moder knows I vill be coming. I vill call her ahead of time.

Sure. I will tell my mother. That would be great.

I vill be avay for a few days, but I vill check on you vhen I return. Okay?

Yes, see you next week, I responded, trying to suppress my excitement.

I immediately ran home to tell my mother what had just happened with Mr. Olchinski, hoping she would not be too angry.

Ma, Mr. Olchinski said he would teach me to play his card game, I told her as I hurried through our kitchen door from the back porch. *He says he would like to come over and give me a lesson next week. He'll call you ahead of time. Doesn't that sound great?*

Oy, Hanele, who told you to invite him to my house? she replied. *I don't tink it's such a good idea.*

Why, ma? It's just a game of cards, that's all. But she knew that I had something else up my sleeve, and it had to do with her. She seemed to have a sixth sense about everything, and my face was always too transparent.

Vhen he call next veek, I gonna tink about it. Okay? she responded with a skeptical look.

That sounds good. Thanks, ma, I responded, holding in my elation.

It was the most I could have hoped for. She did not say absolutely no. There was still a possibility I could get them together. My euphoria at the thought of having Mr. Olchinski in our apartment and seeing him and my mother even talking was almost unbearable. I went into my bedroom, and as I lay on my bed, burying my head in the bed covers, I kicked my toes into the mattress in delight.

Mr. Olchinski had a brother, a survivor of the war, who owned and operated a small general store in Detroit, Michigan. Since the brothers had apparently seen each other only once since the war's end, Mr. Olchinski wanted to fly out to Detroit to spend a week with his brother and his family. I looked forward to seeing him when he returned and thought of him the whole time he was away like a lovesick fan.

A week later, as I walked down the narrow sidewalk on the side of our building leading to the street, I passed Mrs. Burman's apartment and heard loud sobbing. I looked through her window and saw her crying, wiping her eyes with a white handkerchief, crocheted lace surrounding its perimeter. I was hesitant to approach her to ask why she was weeping, but when I heard her mention Mr. Olchinski's name, I had to know the reason. Mr. Olchinski was always on my mind.

I walked in through her open door and walked toward her as she sat on one of her comfortable upholstered living room chairs. Her *zoftig* body was resting at the tip of the seat as though it were either in the process of standing up or sitting down.

Is there something I can do to help you, Mrs. Burman? I can tell that you are very upset.

It's okay, Hanele. I just heard some bad news, dat's all.

Does it have to do with Mr. Olchinski? I thought I heard his name.

Yes, Hanele, she replied hesitatingly, *I'm so sorry to be da von to tell you dat Mr. Olchinski is . . . er iz toyt* [he is dead], she blurted out, as she wiped her nose with the handkerchief and took a deep breath.

What do you mean? He's not dead. He can't be dead.

Yes. He vas vit his broder in da store and a robber came in and shot dem. Da broder is still in da hospital, but Vladek, I mean Mr. Olchinski, vas already toyt. I'm really so sorry to be da von to tell you. Oy, it's such a shame.

The air felt thick and suffocating around me as I fought to keep from collapsing to the ground in anguish. My temples were pounding so loud after Mrs. Burman uttered the word *toyt* that I almost could not hear her as she told me of the terrible incident that had taken Mr. Olchinski's life. An innocent visit to his sibling had resulted in the most gruesome violence. A voice in my head kept repeating, *He was supposed to teach me his card game. He was supposed to visit us in our apartment. He was supposed to marry my mother. How could this be?*

Then, my subconscious asserted itself, pushing aside my conscious self, I said, *You know, Mrs. Burman, I never told anybody this, but I was hoping maybe someday he would marry my mother.*

She looked at me with a combination of surprise and sympathy in her eyes and said, *Oy, Hanele. I hope you vill understand, but Mr. Olchinski vould never marry your moder. He vas looking for a younger voman vit no children, but he never found her.*

Oh, I see. Well, please don't tell anybody about my little secret. I just thought about it, you know, but I wasn't really serious.

I understand, Hanele. Don't vorry, I von't tell anyvon.

Children in my community usually did not accompany their parents to funerals unless the deceased was a member of their own family. However, in this case, I asked my mother if I could attend, and she consented. I suspect she understood my intense emotions about Mr. Olchinski's death and knew I wanted to witness his final chapter on earth.

Ironically, Mr. Rosenlicht, who had given me the private furtive warning about Mr. Olchinski's character, did not appear at the funeral. I saw him only outside the gates of the cemetery, my first experience at a sacred burial ground. As a descendent of Moses' brother Aaron, who was conferred the status of *Kohen* (the priest of the nation of Israel in ancient times), Mr. Rosenlicht was forbidden from entering a cemetery. Adhering to strict purity laws, which forbade priests' contact with a corpse to prevent ritual defilement, Mr. Rosenlicht could look only from afar, outside the cemetery's perimeter, as the burial proceeded. As I glanced at him, I saw that he was holding on to the fence's spires, as though he were a prisoner looking out of his cell. I could feel his eyes focused directly on me as I stood watching the coffin lowered into the earth. I was not sure whether his stare was one of compassion or vindication.

Even though my vision of one day having Mr. Olchinski for a father was destroyed, I mourned for him. I missed his handsome presence and grieved for my childish fantasy about a charming prince enhancing my life. Yet, at the same time, a part of me harbored anger for a man who would easily have snubbed me had he lived long enough to find the woman of his dreams — one with no children.

The knowledge of Mr. Olchinski's intentions surely must have been the reason for Mr. Rosenlicht's unexpected admonition. Still, I had to admit that Mr. Olchinski had never led me to think that he had ever been interested in my mother and me in a serious way. He had shown only politeness and courtesy to a young girl who hovered around him like a fruit fly on an overripe melon.

Mr. Olchinski's death ended my quest for a father among the *grine*. I gave up trying to force a happy family on my mother whether she wanted it or not. In a way, it was a relief to cease my hapless efforts at ingratiating myself with uninterested or unwilling potential marriage partners. I surrendered to the fact that my mother had reasons for her intransigent, stubborn attitude and, unfortunately, I would never change her mind.

CHAPTER 42

The "H" Chain

Most of the *grine* families had moved away from the North End by the fall of 1958, leaving my mother and me among the few who remained at our Osgood Street apartment building. Although promotional opportunities were looming at the Victoria Dress Corporation, they had not yet occurred. My mother was not financially secure enough to consider a move to a nicer neighborhood. I moved on from Lincoln Elementary to Chestnut Junior High School, where my circle of friends began to change dramatically.

While many of my cohorts among the *grine* had scattered to other locations within the city, I met a new diverse group of students starting in the seventh grade, when I was eleven years old. I looked forward to seeing Peter and Thomas, best friends whom I had met in my homeroom on the first day of school. Peter was a short, stout boy who wore colorful plaid shirts with khaki pants. He wore a pencil in his shirt pocket and kept another securely stuck in his kinky hair, resting on the top rim of his ear; I wondered whether he had forgotten that he was carrying one of them.

> *Peter, did you know that you have two pencils on you?*
> *Sure, I know. I'm smart. I always like to have a backup pen-*
> *cil I can grab real quick, just in case I lose one of 'em. Good*
> *idea, right?* he said, grabbing his pencil from his ear like the
> quick draw of a pistol from its holster. The smile on his face
> made me unsure whether he was serious or facetious.

Yeah, you know, it really is a good idea, I replied. *I carry extra pencils in my purse, so I guess I'm doing the same thing as you.*

That makes you pretty smart, too, he grinned, *but not as smart as me.*

His best friend, Thomas, was much taller and leaner than Peter, with a more serious demeanor. Yet, when they were together, they made as good a comedy team as Laurel and Hardy, telling jokes, pretending to trip over each other, and teasing me about my rapidly increasing height as I began to tower over most of my classmates. The pranks they pulled, however, did not detract from the fact that they were, indeed, among the smartest students in the school, specializing in mathematics and acting as unofficial math tutors to the rest of us. Peter and Thomas were the first African Americans with whom I had ever interacted in or out of school, yet the issue of race had never entered my mind when I was eleven.

Chestnut Junior High School was a massive, towering structure built at the turn of the twentieth century. Its majestic facade was constructed of yellow brick while tall, white, thick pillars graced its exterior entranceway. The schools I had attended until then ranged from the Lubavitcher Yeshiva, which had been converted from an elegant former residence, to the small neighborhood Lincoln Elementary School. They were both minuscule compared with my seventh-grade educational environment. However, I easily adjusted to the bustle in corridors filled with the din of hundreds of students talking, giggling, and rushing to their classes as soon as each bell rang. Besides Jane and Mandy, the petite sisters who became my best friends and accompanied my mother and me on our weekly weekend visits to Klibanoff's for a corned beef sandwich, not many other Jewish students remained in the section of the city covered by the Chestnut School district.

The old Chestnut Street School, 2009, from the Springfield Republican

It was in my Home Economics class that I met my secret admirer. He was a redheaded, freckle-faced, slightly plump boy who stuck out like a sore thumb in a class normally reserved for girls. Having a boy in sewing class was certainly an odd sight, not the usual haunting grounds for a male student who had the option of attending shop class, the customary venue for boys learning how to construct things with their hands. But there he was, his pattern pieces laid out in front of him, his tracing tool in hand, imprinting the pattern onto the cotton fabric. The teacher allowed him to make a shirt instead of the usual apron all the girls were making, and he seemed serious about the task before him. I remembered that Mr. Stossel, one of the bachelors, had a knack for stitchery as well, creating his ornate, velvet trimmed pillows, so I had a model for a male interested in what was typically a female's realm.

Other than saying hello, Tommy McNamara had never actually spoken to me. Sometimes I noticed him looking my way out of the corner of my eye, but I never had enough nerve to ask him how he liked sewing class or why he ever chose to attend in the first place. We never sat near each other or walked to class together. One day, as I sat down in my assigned seat in sewing class, I saw a long rectangular box wrapped in shiny silver paper dotted with little red hearts on the table before me. My tablemate, Helena, giggled as she watched my surprised, quizzical face.

Is this box for meee? I wonder whether it was put here by mistake because I can't think of anyone who would give me a box like this, I asked incredulously, in a voice that closely resembled a squeal.

Helena replied, *It's for you all right. I saw the person who put it there. He asked me if I was sure this was your seat.*

Really? Wow, who was it? I asked loudly, inadvertently attracting the attention of the girls sitting nearby.

Can't say, she replied. *You'll see when you open the card.*

Then I guess I'd better open it, I said, while, by that point, all the girls in the class looked my way in unison.

After removing the wrapping paper, I opened the box. Inside was a thick, large imitation gold letter "H" linked to an imitation gold-chain necklace. As I placed the chain around my neck, I noticed that the "H" was scuffed on one side where its outer layer was beginning to peel off. Still, the excitement of the moment pushed the slight imperfection out of my mind. Under the box lay a small envelope with my first name printed in bold capital letters on the front, H-A-N-N-A. The card inside was about the size of a business card and read, *To a sweet girl, Tommy.*

He did not approach me to acknowledge his gift after class, nor did I thank him for it. I barely looked at him, embarrassed at receiving something so personal from someone to whom I had never even spoken. The next day I decided to wear the "H" chain around my neck with a new skirt and blouse my mother had created. Observing the necklace, Tommy approached me for the first time at my locker, and said, *That necklace looks really nice on you. I knew it would.*

Thank you for giving it to me, I said softly as we began to walk together to my next class. *I'll try to wear it every day if I can.*

Little conversation ever ensued in school between Tommy and me beyond that point, but the rest of our classmates swiftly identified us as boyfriend and girlfriend, and we never corrected them. I never asked him why he chose home economics over shop class, but I suspected it might have been because it was where the girls were. We were surely the most silent eleven-year-old sweethearts on earth — until my brush with death.

CHAPTER 43

The Fever

My mother never mentioned the "H" chain, even though I began to wear it to school every day. She knew the boy who had given it to me was not Jewish. She also knew my silence regarding the gift's source meant I did not want to talk with her about it. Concerned that opening up the subject of the "H" chain would lead to my mother's criticism, I had decided to leave the topic closed to discussion.

Surprisingly, when a week had passed after I had received the gift, she still had not asked who had given it to me. However, since my mother was notorious for her methodical and deliberate manner, always possessing a reason for her actions, I was certain her calmness was a tactical maneuver to achieve whatever aim she had in mind. For the time being, however, I was content with her silence.

December 1958 was a typically frigid New England time of year. I do not remember an unusual abundance of snow that winter. In fact, as I recollect, it was a particularly dry winter season. After having lived in Massachusetts for almost a decade, I was familiar with the need to dress warmly "in layers" when venturing outside, snowing or not. I wore boots daily on my walk to Chestnut School to keep the chill from my feet. One day, however, dressing in haste and afraid I would be late for school, I neglected to wear my boots, sporting only my penny loafers. Later, the community said that it was this one act of carelessness that led to my debilitating illness.

Winter 1957, on Osgood Street. If only the author had worn these boots the following year!

The cough began in the middle of the night, a constant hacking, keeping me up for several hours. By morning, I had difficulty breathing, severe respiratory congestion, and a fever of 104 degrees. My mother had stayed up with me all night, the look of fear beginning to take shape on her face. She called the doctor's office in the morning as soon as it opened. Dr. Newmark, the pediatrician who had tuned me into the facts of life, was favored by most of the *grine* because of his willingness to make house calls and because of his caring bedside manner. He hastened to visit me at home later in the morning and quickly offered his diagnosis: pneumonia.

I was too sick to be fearful, too occupied with gasping for breath, but my mother's face told me my condition was extremely serious. Her obstinate face also told me she would be damned if she would let go of the one thing that kept her going, the one thing that made her life worthwhile — the child who would bring her family forward into the future.

> *I think it would be a good idea to transfer your daughter to the hospital, Mrs. Perlstein,* Dr. Newmark advised. *She'll get good care there.*
>
> *Please, Dr. Newmark, please let me keep her at home. I can take care on her. I vill stay home every day mit her. If she get too sick, I promise I vill let her go to da hospital,* my mother pleaded.
>
> *All right, I will allow you to keep her home for now. But if her condition worsens in any way, I will demand that she be transferred to the hospital. No questions asked,* he said.
>
> *Okay, I agree.*

The doctor had prescribed antibiotics several times during the day along with decongestants and aspirin to bring my fever down. A makeshift oxygen tent was erected around my bed. Although I cannot recall how it was constructed, the enhanced oxygen to my lungs and tissues and ultimately my bloodstream was a welcome relief.

My recovery was slow. The first few days were harrowing and unpredictable as my fever seesawed dramatically for a while, sometimes lulling us into thinking it was permanently down, only to shoot back up a few hours later. Seeing my mother's worried face, I could tell she was mulling over the possibility of calling Dr. Newmark and acceding to his suggestion of admitting me to the hospital.

A number of my caretakers, like Mrs. Kester, Mrs. Landsman, and Mrs. Lott, came to see how I was doing, standing beside my oxygenated bed, their apprehensive faces obvious. My mother sat with them in the kitchen sipping glasses of tea, discussing my distressed condition, and receiving comfort and support from her cohorts. I wondered whether, as usual, all four had shared the same teabag, each dipping it quickly into their cup of boiling water and passing it on in succession to save it for future use. One teabag could easily handle six or seven cups of tea if it were only dipped and not steeped.

> *A gogel mogel, dat's vhat she needs,* advised Mrs. Landsman, as I sat up again in my bed to cough. *Dat vill help da cough and sore troat. Do you have some eggs, Mrs. Perilshtein?*
>
> *A gogel mogel, such a good idea,* said Mrs. Kester. *I make it all da time.*
>
> *Noting vorks better den a gogel mogel,* chimed in Mrs. Lott.
>
> *Vell, I have eggs in da frigidaire,* my mother announced, using the brand name to refer to all refrigerators.
>
> *Let me have dem, and I vill make a gogel mogel right now,* Mrs. Landsman replied emphatically.

My mother took out the carton of eggs and presented it on the kitchen table to Mrs. Landsman, who, as the best chef around, knew how to concoct an old European remedy for the relief of a cough and congestion. Her recipe was simple: two egg yolks briskly mixed with three or four teaspoons of sugar, the simplest form of the medicine, with no added flavorings or hard liquor. The result was a thick yellow fusion of the sweet and the wholesome, a little thinner in consistency than cake batter.

> *Svallow et in von shluk* [one gulp], *Hanele,* my mother appealed, offering me the magic potion in a glass.

Although a *gogel mogel* was not a favorite remedy for many of the *grine* children, I happened to like the taste and drank it down quickly, as prescribed. I was unable to swallow any other food.

On the second day of my illness, my mother answered the phone and heard a boy's voice.

Hello.

Hello, you must be Hanna's mother. My name is Tommy, and I was wondering how she is doing. The kids at school told me she is pretty sick. Can I talk to her?

No, I am sorry. She can't talk on da phone yet. Maybe in a few days you can talk to her. I vill tell her you called. Goodbye.

After the call, she came to my bed, and said, *Tommy call you to see how you are. I tell him he can call again vhen you are able to talk. Okay?*

Thanks, ma, I said, while thinking, *Is she ever going to reprimand me for having a non-Jewish "boyfriend?" Why is she being so hard to read? What's going on in her head?*

On the fourth day, I no longer needed the oxygen tent, which made communication a lot easier. However, I still had a fever, albeit lower, a troublesome cough, and an aching body, largely a result of the strain of nonstop coughing. I was generally in a weakened state, but I could tell I was improving. My mother's face had softened from its constricted, mournful visage during the first few days of my ailment to one of obvious relief. My illness was still far from over, but the critical days seemed to be behind me. Able to walk around a little bit, I went into the kitchen for a cup of tea. Sure enough, a used dry teabag rested on a tea stained plate at the center of the kitchen table. I boiled some water in a teakettle, poured it into a cup, and dipped the teabag into it, placing it back onto the plate for the next tea drinker. Who knows how many dips it had endured at that point?

Tommy had called every day since his first contact, and my mother had continued to deny him the opportunity to talk to me until the sixth day. On that day, without warning, she gave me the phone and said, *It's Tommy, for you.*

During the rest of my illness, I talked with Tommy every day on the phone about how I was, what I was missing at school, our sewing teacher, and the antics of some of our classmates. It was not much of a conversation, but it was more than we had ever talked in the past when I was present at school.

It took almost three weeks for me to feel well enough to return to school and resume my everyday life. As I needed to catch up on many of my studies, both at Chestnut and my Hebrew school, I did not have much time available to socialize for a while. Tommy and I drifted apart over the course of the rest of the seventh grade, although I am not sure we had ever been together in the first place. By the end of the school year, I had misplaced the "H" chain, whose outer surface had begun to chip even further, and never found it again.

My mother had played her cards strategically for a nonparticipating card player. She would be opposed to any serious relationship with a non-Jew in the future, when I was older, a firm believer of remaining with the faith and holding with tradition. Yet, when I was eleven, she knew it was way too early to worry about my future marital plans. Furthermore, the reassuring phone calls helped to lift my spirits and probably hastened my recovery. She had decided to remain calm and let my early love life unfold as she had anticipated it would.

CHAPTER 44

The Promotion

After having spent most of the 1950s at the Victoria Dress Corporation as a sewing machine operator, my mother had shown everyone there her special talents as a seamstress. She knew not only how to sew ladies garments swiftly and accurately, but she also knew every component of the sewing machine from the bobbin to the needle plate to the presser foot to the motor. Mr. Podell, the owner, knew she was ready to take over as a manager at the factory to join the supervisor in overseeing the workers and the whole operation. She was relieved of her seat at the sewing machine and promoted to forewoman in 1959.

> *Hanele, guess vhat?* she said as she arrived home on the day of her promotion. *I gonna be da forevoman at da shop! Isn't dat someting?*
>
> *Wow, ma. This is one of the most exciting days ever.*
>
> *Yeh. Mr. Podell say he vill pay me $125 every veek. I never see so much money in my life. It's just mazel,* she added, using the Yiddish word for "luck" in her familiar accented voice.
>
> *No, it's not just luck, ma. You gotta know that your sewing is so much better than anyone else in the world. It really is,* I said, with tears in my eyes.

I had never been as proud of my mother as the day she announced her promotion. Her face expressed much joy and pride at being recognized for her work and for the move up in rank and salary. To us, $125 a week may as well have been $1,000. It could not have made us any happier. It held out the promise of good things happening to us in the future. Still, I was worried about how my mother would remain on her feet all day in the new job. She had cried out in pain often during my childhood, her throbbing legs causing her to lie down soon after returning home from work. I hoped she would find a way to perform her new duties without worsening her precarious physical condition.

Taking advantage of her new position, she began to put in a good word for other members of the *grine* at the dress factory, recommending them for employment. Within a short time, several of them came to work at the Victoria Dress factory. Knowledge of dressmaking was common in our community, and my mother knew that those she had recommended could do the work. At that time, I had no doubt in my mind that my mother would have a home at the company for as long as she wanted it. Mr. Podell would always protect and safeguard her job, I thought, because my mother was the absolute best at producing well-made ladies garments.

Little did we know then, the forewoman's job would last only a few more years. When Mr. Podell retired later, in the 1960s, the supervisor bought the company. My mother's future as the forewoman was cut short when the new owner decided he no longer needed her services. At first, she had a hard time adjusting to the loss of her job after fourteen years, almost to the point of exasperation. She took to her bed for a time, unable to fathom her severance. However, the experience served as a stepping-stone to my mother beginning a self-owned enterprise, exposing her skill with a thread and needle to thousands of customers and onlookers around western New England starting in the mid-1960s.

Similar rumblings of moving up the economic ladder occurred all around us among the *grine*. For example, Mr. Feldman had saved

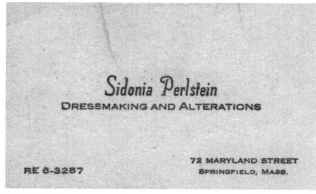

Sidonia's business card

enough money to buy an appliance repair business and began to acquire customers. Mr. Feinberg transformed his door-to-door sales business into a larger scale operation, gaining big companies as accounts. Mr. Bach began to invest in real estate. The Skalrz brothers opened a successful sheet metal business, and Mr. Zagruder was accepted as a student at a local college and studied to become an accountant while keeping his job at the men's coat factory. It seemed that at least the men among the *grine* were improving their economic foothold in America.

Most of the women, however, as was typical of that time in American history, were not able to move into more lucrative careers and continued to work at their usual jobs as cooks, seamstresses, and hospital workers. My mother was fortunate to have a champion like Mr. Podell to support her talent and boost her income.

The late 1950s and early 1960s was the period when our immigrant group made its initial attempts at making its economic mark on American society. Only a decade after their arrival on American shores, the *grine* were already making inroads into their new world, and there was no turning back.

CHAPTER 45

The Big Move

In the late summer of 1959, ten years after having come to Springfield, my mother and I were scheduled to move to a new apartment in the Forest Park neighborhood of Springfield. I had heard about the apartment when I returned from Kansas City after having spent the summer there with one of my mother's only surviving first cousins, Olga, and her family. I felt much more grown up when I came back after having been away from my mother and familiar surroundings, meeting new cousins close to my own age, and experiencing my first kiss with a boy. On the verge of turning twelve, I felt mature enough to move to a two-family house in a new neighborhood.

Although our transportation in 1959 was limited since we did not yet own a car, my mother and I had traveled with others to various sections of Springfield. We were familiar with other areas of the city, like the Forest Park neighborhood, the South End, Maple and Mulberry Streets, Indian Orchard, Hungry Hill, and Pine Point. Remembering our drives through those neighborhoods, we often appraised the features of each home and wondered about their cost. Like many American families, my mother and I had dreamed that one day we might own our own place. When the possibility arose, however, it was not that simple.

When my mother told me about the impending move, she also confided that she had visited a house for sale during my absence. It was a small cape with two bedrooms on a small lot, just big enough for the two of us. Having received the promotion to forewoman at the Victoria Dress Corporation just a few months earlier, she was in a much better financial position and could afford a home. However, she had hesitated buying it because she was "*a voman alone*" and because she was not sure she could manage the responsibility of maintaining her own home.

> *I vanted to tell you den ve vould have our own house, but I just couldn't do it*, she said wistfully, as though she harbored significant regret about not having taken the risk.
>
> *Can you change your mind now, ma? Can I go and see it?* I asked. *Gee, it would be so nice to have a place that was only ours*, I sighed, disappointed that she had made the decision without consulting me.
>
> She looked down at the floor as though she had let me down. Upon seeing me return from my summer sojourn in Kansas City and looking me in the face, she seemed to have had a change of heart about the whole matter.
>
> *I so sorry, Hanele, but da house vas sold to somevon else. Ve missed our chance. It's not so good an idea to see it now.*
>
> *Ma, it's okay. I'm still looking forward to moving to the new neighborhood anyway.*

We had missed the chance to own a home, and the opportunity never came up again. We were destined to rent space in someone else's property for the rest of our life together.

By the end of the 1950s, we joined most of the rest of the *grine* who had moved away from the North End and Osgood Street. We occupied our new space on the second floor of a two-family home owned by Lazar and Beatrice Stambovsky on Maryland Street, near the old zoo entrance.

Our Forest Park home, 2011

The Landsmans, after having experienced their own move to a place a few blocks away, used their pickup truck to help us move our few belongings to the new address just a week before I started the eighth grade at Forest Park Junior High School.

Although the bedrooms were smaller than those in our Osgood Street apartment, the new place had an extra room near the outside porch where my mother could set up her new sewing room. Her sewing supplies, such as her machine, our old formica-topped kitchen table that served as her cutting surface, her ironing board topped with a water-filled measuring cup, and a bookcase holding remnants and bolts of fabrics and a multitude of patterns, took up all the space in the room. It was set up so naturally with all her necessary sewing items that it seemed as though we had always had a similar room in our former apartment. I believe my mother had already envisioned the dedicated sewing room as the key to the future enterprise she would initiate in the next decade.

CHAPTER 46

The Debut

The official debut of my mother's fashions occurred in the spring of 1960, when I was twelve, the year following our move to Forest Park. Although I have recalled this event many times before, I have never viewed it completely from my mother's perspective. This is how I imagine she planned to formally unveil her fashion acumen.

After having received an invitation to the biggest bar mitzvah we had ever attended, my mother knew that my appearance, wearing one of her signature designer dresses, would expose her skills to many potential customers. Because of my mother's self-imposed isolation, we did not receive too many invitations to special parties and events, so this one, with its large guest list, could not have been any more opportune. I had already reached my full height at that point, five feet eight inches, and had developed a lean but shapely figure. The dress I wore to the event would be the most important dress my mother would ever produce.

It had to be a garment that would create a buzz among the guests over the exquisite qualities of its design, its detailing, and its fit. In other words, it had to be perfect. My mother saw this occasion as the ideal forum for society to take notice of her: her debut. If the dress were to achieve the response she sought, she could launch her new business.

What was it like to be a single mother in a new country with no family at a time when such status was scorned? It was lonely, uncertain, and at times humiliating. In the 1950s, most people attached a stigma to parents without spouses. Single parents in those days were either widows or, to a lesser extent, divorcees, but my mother was neither. As is the case today, many single mothers had great difficulty earning an adequate income to support their families unless they were highly educated. Lacking education, a woman would have to possess a singular talent that could propel her to public recognition for her skill and attract people in a positive way. My mother yearned for that positive public recognition, and she knew how to obtain it.

As she had hoped and dreamed, the white raw silk dress with bateau neckline, bouffant sleeves, full skirt, and narrow gold belt was an immediate sensation. Every woman, and many of the men, commented on the magnificence of the garment. I stood out among the hundreds of female guests at the reception. In contrast, my mother's dress, true to her self-effacing manner, was a simple white cotton short-sleeved frock that allowed her to stay in the background and let all observers focus on her daughter's outstanding designer outfit.

> *Oy, Hanele, du bist azoy sheyn* [you are so beautiful], *an vhat a dress!* Many of the women told me.
> *Your moder is really someting to make dis dress. Just vonderful. Keynehore* [No evil eye], they all said, employing the traditional Yiddish comment when wishing someone the best, but avoiding any infliction of an evil eye, the dreaded *nehore*. To say *keynehore* was a compliment and a warning at the same time, to ward off any lurking curse from the recipient of the praise.

Our lives were never the same after this watershed event. Word of the gorgeous dress spread to others in our neighborhood and across the city. My mother was still working at the Victoria Dress

The author and her friend Brigitta dancing at the big bar mitzvah, 1960

Corporation, but she transformed her home fashions into more sophisticated designs after the raw silk dress, setting the stage for her eventual emergence as an entrepreneur. Being able to work from home with an opportunity to rest when needed was a welcome benefit.

After the debut, as I entered my adolescent years, I began to view myself with a new confidence and esteem I had not possessed earlier. The accolades I received wearing the raw silk dress and, more important, my mother's approval of my graceful bearing in showcasing it, changed me. Although I was unaware of it at the time, my mother had achieved her twofold goal of gaining positive recognition for her rare skill and boosting her daughter's self-assurance and poise.

My mother would never again accuse me of appearing *farkrimpte* (standing crooked). *Dat's right, Hanele, never forget, you stand up straight.*

CHAPTER 47

The Car

With the exception of such large metropolitan areas as New York City, where an extensive, large-scale transportation system is in place, it is hard to imagine living in most parts of America without an automobile. Yet many Americans are still forced to do just that. They rely on the kindness of others, public transportation, or their feet to take them where they need to go.

Twelve years after our arrival in the United States, my mother purchased her first car. Until then, she had taken the city bus to the Victoria Dress Corporation on William Street in the South End of Springfield since she was hired in 1951. The city bus also took us downtown to shopping areas outside our neighborhood, sometimes just one way. We relied on our feet to take the long walk home. Occasionally, one of the *grine* who owned a car would drive us to places of recreation, joining other members of our community. A growing collection of Ford Fairlanes and Chevy Bel Airs began to dot the street near our block by the late 1950s. As I recollect, my mother was among the last members of our community to invest in an automobile.

As with the house she had been fearful of purchasing a couple years earlier, my mother was hesitant about buying a car. It seemed a complicated machine with strange parts: a transmission, tires, hoses, a battery, and various other components totally unfamiliar to her and requiring care and attention. She was at home with a sewing machine, so she knew a bit about motors, but a car seemed beyond her scope of comprehension. Although she was afraid of it, she had saved enough money to purchase a vehicle and knew it was the most practical step to take at that moment in her life. She was willing to take the plunge, but it had to be a new car, not someone else's former possession, which may have had maintenance or repair problems in the past. That would have been too worrisome.

Mr. Sklarz offered to take my mother and me to the Chevy dealer in the early fall of 1961 and to sit with us as my mother negotiated a deal for the car she desired. I was never sure whether she wanted him to come with her because he was more knowledgeable about automobiles or because he was a man. As a woman, she understood the advantage of having a man along to discuss transactions for such things as cars and tools and houses. She was a keen observer of how people related to one another, and when it came to the purchase of big-ticket items, her intuition told her it was a good idea to be accompanied by a man.

In the end, her negotiations unfolded like this:

I am interested in da Chevy Impela, she told the auto sales associate.

You mean the Chevy Impala, he replied politely, correcting her mispronunciation of his product.

Yes.

Did you like the one we just test drove? It was a four-door V-8 with that handsome white stripe on the side.

I don't know. It vas maybe too fancy for me.

I can offer you a good price for the one we just drove. The sticker price is $2,697, but because we'll be coming out with the 1962 models pretty soon, I can sell it to you for $2,600. That's the best I could do. It's a really great price.

Mr. Sklarz was about to interject with a question or comment, but my mother started to respond anyway, placing her hand on his arm.

> *You know, I tink it's too much for me. Vhat about $2,500 and ve'll drive it avay right now.*
>
> *Sorry, no. I can't let go of that car for anything less than $2,600. There are a lot of people interested in that car. It's the most popular one in our showroom. No, can't do it.*
>
> *Okay, vell, ve gonna go now. Maybe it's not a good time for me to buy a car. Come, Mr. Sklarz, let's go, an you too Hanele,* she said, as she grabbed my hand. Her action was so abrupt, the salesman did not have an opportunity to say anything to stop her from leaving.

We were already outside the dealership when the salesman called us back and said he would be willing to talk to his manager about adjusting the price. My mother pretended to whisper to Mr. Sklarz about I do not know what as they sat back down in the salesman's partitioned office.

> When the salesman returned, he said quietly, probably hoping no one could hear him, *I spoke with the manager. You've got it for $2,500. You can have the one in the showroom.*
>
> *Tank you. Ve'll take it,* she replied stoically, not giving away any of the emotion she must have been feeling inside.

All this occurred without Mr. Sklarz ever getting to say a word, but he had an appreciative grin on his face, recognizing a true *handler* when he saw one.

The 1961 Chevy Impala was the first car of only three my mother owned for the rest of her long life. Besides her sewing machine, she loved that car more than anything else she had ever purchased in America. It gave her the freedom and flexibility she had always craved. Learning to drive and earning a driver's license at the age of forty-eight was a real accomplishment for anyone, especially a woman who initially approached car ownership with great apprehension.

The car and the license to drive were my mother's tickets to real independence and empowerment, allowing her to venture out to places she had never seen — on her own terms and timetable. She felt well on her way to achieving the American dream.

CHAPTER 48

Restitution: The Meandering Conclusion

While my mother's restitution case was initiated in the mid-1950's, when we still lived on Osgood Street, the seemingly never-ending legal matter with the West German government tested my mother's resolve and determination to achieve rightful recompense for a very long time. As she succeeded in her attempts to assimilate into American life, she still had to deal with the injustices of her former life. Long after we had made our move from the North End to Forest Park, my mother continued to confront the rejections relating to her claim for reparation.

As a freshman in college, I was often not with my mother in the mid-1960s when these letters arrived in her mailbox. Yet, she always kept me apprised of her restitution case and displayed her determination to continue the process. When I returned home to visit her, the tension and anxiety in her face were so frightening that I begged her to stop her pursuit, accept the offers, and close her case. My protection instincts emerged with a fury.

> *Please, ma, I can't stand seeing you so upset. Just close the case and forget about it,* I said.

My plea produced a long, achingly painful response: *I sorry, Hanele, I just cen't do it. My family, dey vould vant me to keep going, to get vhat is fair, Hani. I am not da same person as vhen I vas home. My whole life is changed. Everyting vas taken avay from me — mayn koyakh ['my strength,' but*

*meaning 'health'], my family, Laurie. All I have is you. You are
everyting to me now. I hope you vill understand,* she replied,
with uncommon tears in her eyes.

I don't understand, ma. I really don't, I responded emphat-
ically, my voice rising. *If you keep this case going, your nervousness and depression will just get worse.*

Maybe, but I have no oder vay. Dat's it.

Of course, *dat's it* meant the conversation was over. Interestingly,
much to my consternation, these findings coincided with the time
my mother severed her ties with the Victoria Dress Corporation,
where, at this point, she had worked for the previous fourteen years.
Although her income was at one of its all-time lows, she still vowed
to continue her fight. Anyway, I had to get back to my classes, so I
put any thoughts about her compensation case aside for the time
being. But the matter was still front and center for my mother, who,
apparently, in 1966, hired a German translator to assist in interpret-
ing letters with counsel at the URO. Before the translator began his
work, the following letter arrived in English:

September 8, 1965

Dear Mrs. Perlstein,

*. . . I received now the decision according to which the
appeal was rejected. . . . A new appeal against this decision
is not permitted and there is nothing more we can do in this
matter. I regret to have to give you such disappointing news.*

Sincerely yours,
Dr. R. Mendelsohn

Yet another year passed, and another letter arrived from the URO
— this time addressed to my mother's local German intermediary,
Leonard Hamlisch:

April 13, 1966

Dear Mr. Hamlisch:

   In the matter of Mrs. Perlstein . . . the injury to health has been lost in all instances. . . . An appeal will not be approved. . . . The client did not submit a nervous complaint, and up to 1964 no nervous complaint from a physician was mentioned. Mrs. Perlstein only declared a nervous complaint after refusal of the injury–to–health case. . . .

Sincerely yours,
Dr. R. Mendelsohn

Mr. Hamlisch lost no time in conveying his forceful reply, dated the next day:

April 14, 1966

Dear Mr. Mendelsohn,

   Thank you for your letter, but, unfortunately, I cannot agree with you. I have a letter from the URO dated September 7, 1960, copy enclosed, in which it states, in paragraph two, that the nervous complaint was acknowledged and costs for that would be paid. . . . The first doctor's report that my client submitted was from Dr. Freund of Springfield, Massachusetts, who stated the nervous condition in detail in his certificate. . . .

   Mrs. Perlstein told me today that the consulate doctor . . . in Worcester, never examined her at all, but referred her to a foot specialist.

   In the past, it was difficult to achieve compensation for a nervous complaint, the situation has changed in recent years, and I ask you for the new procedure for taking possible legal action.

. . . I await your response with great interest.

Sincerely yours,
Leonard Hamlisch

This was a swift and masterful rebuttal to the negative appeal, pointing out the apparently overlooked previous reports about my mother's ongoing mental health complaints. Having an expert in the German language helping her to translate the legal documents and provide legal advice may have been a welcome comfort to her in coping with the maze of bureaucracy that was the German compensation authority.

Two months later, my mother's intermediary wrote in exasperation:

June 28, 1966
In reference to my letter of April 14, 1966

Dear Dr. Mendelsohn,
Regarding the above letter I have not received an answer as of today. . . . The woman is very nervous and went again to a specialist. See the enclosed certificate.
Since the time for following up will expire in August, I strongly request that you communicate with me regarding whether you will continue the case or not...

At the bottom of Mr. Hamlisch's letter appears a heartbreaking plea from my mother, written in German, most certainly with assistance in grammar from her intermediary:

Dear Doctor,
It is at my instigation that the above letter was written expressing my wishes. I must just once see clearly and do not

wish to have the case further delayed. At this point, I await
your decision.

Sincerely yours,
Sidonia Perlstein

The enclosed opinion of the local specialist, Dr. Walter Penino, was
as follows: *Severe nervous tension . . . has been present over many*
years. . . . The tension displayed . . . is far beyond that seen in the aver-
age 'nervous individual.' . . . She has experienced recurrent headaches
that have frequently incapacitated her. . . . Consider her to be at least
fifty percent incapacitated at the present time.

Six months later:

December 7, 1966

Dear Mr. Hamlisch:
*   In the absence of Dr. Mendelsohn . . . I have taken on the*
case. . . . A motion based on Paragraph 35 must be based on
the fact that the established illness has so deteriorated that a
claim for a monthly pension is warranted. . . . Dr. Penino must
highlight the symptoms and incorporate them in his report . . .
It would have been good if he could have submitted a detailed
report in his previous two letters. . . . Perhaps it is possible for
Dr. Penino to clarify the case. . . .

Sincerely yours,
Dr. K. Bachman

Shortly thereafter, the following:

January 20, 1967

Dear Mr. Hamlisch:
*   I am confirming receipt of the new report from Dr. Penino.*
I have to tell you again, unfortunately, that I don't think that

kind of report will be sufficient. . . .

I now ask you whether you think Dr. Penino will provide another report . . . in which he can indicate whether Mrs. Perlstein's condition in the course of the last two years has substantially deteriorated. . . . If this is not possible…I can already say that a successful outcome will hardly be possible…

The report must be in the German language, that is to say, with translation provided. . . .

Sincerely yours,
Dr. K. Bachman

Two days later Mr. Hamlisch wrote:

January 22, 1967

Regarding your letter, I would like to ask you to send me another letter in "English" at the same time as a draft of the certificate. . . . The local doctor doesn't understand what you need on the certificate. . . . I had your recent letter translated, but I have not yet seen the translation. However, I don't believe [the certificate] will be correct.

Sincerely yours,
Leonard Hamlisch

The correspondence stopped for a while, or perhaps the documents are missing from my saved files, but it is easy to determine that the case was rejected again a time or two during the next year, when the following unexpected letter arrived:

March 5, 1968

Dear Mr. Hamlisch:
The files are still in the hands of the medical officials in Hannover. We can determine that the report of Dr. Brunt

and Dr. Meiger is positive and an overall reduction due to the persecution is established between 32 and 37%.

Now we must wait for the opinion of the medical officials in Hannover, which, experience shows, takes a longer time. We have the case under control. . . .

Sincerely yours,
Dr. K. Bachman

Less than two months later, however, the final decision of the board came, incredibly, to a different conclusion:

April 29, 1968

Dear Mr. Hamlisch:

We have received the ruling of the compensation authority. The deterioration request was rejected. Essentially, the board's case is based on the fact that the diagnosis of Dr. Meiger and Dr. Brunt was already established at the time of the first examination in 1960, and that at that time, she was evaluated at 20%, and then, during the whole proceedings, no nervous complaint was mentioned, and on the contrary, when the findings were presented, the condition of the client improved rather than worsened.

Against this opinion, the authority must establish that the follow-up examination of Dr. Meiger and Dr. Brunt in September 1967 established the degree of reduction of work ability at 30% and that the reduction of work ability from that day should have been estimated at 30%.

You can present an appeal. . . .

Sincerely yours,
Dr. K. Bachman

A month later, the representative of the URO tried, at the behest of Mr. Hamlisch, to clarify his own concerns about the compensation board's April decision:

May 22, 1968

Dear Mr. Hamlisch:
. . . We corresponded in our letter of April 29 [as to] why the decision of the authority did not seem right. The authority did not say in its opinion even once that it had asked its own consulting physician about this matter. The result of an appeal cannot be predicted and it remains up to Mrs. Perlstein whether she wants to present an appeal or not. . . .

Sincerely yours,
Dr. K. Bachman

By the end of 1969, my mother and Mr. Hamlisch seemed to have parted ways for unknown reasons. He may have resigned from a case that had been in a circling pattern for years. In November 1969, a letter arrived addressed directly to my mother referring to dates heretofore not mentioned, but for medical complaints that dated back up to a dozen years:

November 11, 1969

Dear Mrs. Perlstein:
We calculate that you are entitled for the period from January 1, 1958 – December 31, 1968 . . . for an application for treatment reimbursement for these acknowledged conditions:
Chronic gall bladder disease
Uprooting depression caused by the persecution
Damaged teeth

Under the terms of the ordinance, the German authority must have all the information perfectly completed by, at the latest, December 31, 1969. . . .

Sincerely,
Dr. K. Bachman

But then, as usual:

November 20, 1969

Dear Mrs. Perlstein:
    In the matter of an appeal, a court session has been ordered for February 6, 1970.

Sincerely,
Dr. K. Bachman

More than a year passed, and apparently, having received another rejection of her mental health appeal, my mother requested a psychiatric examination by another psychiatrist to rebut a negative report by the German consulate physician. The URO sent a letter to the new psychiatrist:

February 17, 1971

Dear Dr. Finkelman,
    Mrs. Sidonia Perlstein . . . instructed us to send you the enclosed medical reports from Dr. Bluger, who performed a medical examination as consulate physician and who found the nerve ailments from which Mrs. Perlstein is suffering now are in no causal connection with her persecution.

*We must have any rebutting report of yours by the end of
the month...*

Sincerely yours,
Dr. K. Bachman

It was baffling how a contented young woman living in a small
rural village in Hungary surrounded by a loving family before the
war could turn into a taciturn, secretive, anxiety-ridden insomniac
afterward. Yet, the consulate physician could still declare, "The
nerve ailments from which Mrs. Perlstein is suffering are in no
causal connection with her persecution."

Despite the new psychiatrist, her appeal was to no avail. She was
never able to prove her long-term mental health disability. By 1973,
at sixty years old, worn down by the German legal process and in
desperate need of funds, she had given up her appeals, accepting
some form of settlement, at least for payment of medical costs:

July 30, 1973

Dear Mrs. Perlstein:
*For the purpose of paying off the sum of DM 3,800 to you
in granted settlement, a "certificate of life," must be submitted.
I am sending you the enclosed for you to complete and signed
by a Notary Public. . . .*

Sincerely yours,
Dr. K. Bachman

The dollar equivalent of DM 3,800 in 1973 averaged $1,434,
depending on the value of the deutsche mark (DM). To receive it, a
signature and notarization on a *proof of life* certificate was required
to prove that the recipient was still alive.

Sixteen years later, in 1989, ridden with guilt at not understanding my mother's pursuit of a just remuneration, I attempted to reopen her case. I thought my intervention might cause the German Indemnification Office to reverse their incongruous decisions, and provide her with a medical pension. The first response from the URO was deflating:

April 30, 1990

Mrs. Hanna Perlstein Marcus
Dear Mrs. Marcus:
. . . Finally, our office in Frankfurt [has] located the file and checked it carefully. The conclusion . . . [is that] there is no chance to accomplish any positive result by filing an application to reopen the original filed application for [a] pension . . . Sorry for the disappointment . . .

Sincerely yours,
H. Hindenberg

By then, I was almost as determined as my mother to pursue her compensation case. As she aged, it seemed the toll of her painful experiences grew more pronounced. She began to whimper when I left her on her own; she imagined each of my days and wondered whether I were safe every moment until I called to reassure her; her nightmares had all but replaced the former pleasant dreams of her childhood. Her depression had finally enveloped her as though she were in an invisible cocoon. Could I not find some measure of justice for her tortured soul?

I hired an attorney in Germany to see if he could assist in re-opening her case to somehow reverse the judgment.

July 10, 1992

> *Dear Mrs. Perlstein,*
>
> *I have seen your compensation files. . . . You can reopen your case for a compensation pension if you can show that your conditions due to the persecution have reached a reduction in your work ability, evaluated at 30%...Only a deterioration of these conditions will restore your previous case. . . . You should obtain a certificate from a new physician.*
>
> *With kind regards,*
> *Dr. Kermit Newman, Attorney*

Almost twenty years had passed, and the same rhetoric was repeated. But I had become equally as adamant as my mother about continuing the case.

Therefore, we found a new psychiatrist in New Haven, and both of us attended several sessions with our newly discovered champion. Dr. Dori Laub was the first of all the physicians my mother had seen throughout her legal ordeal that truly listened to her. A child survivor himself, he understood my mother's mental condition and the experiences that had brought them about. In his comforting presence, she was able to express her aloneness over the fifty years since the murder of her family, and especially since the death of her sister, Laura, who had traveled with her to three concentration camps before she died of typhus, only two months before the liberation of the Bergen Belsen camp.

My mother's words about me, spoken to Dr. Laub in his office: *She da von who help me be a mentsch, to make a life here. If I didn't have her, I couldn't survive,* changed my view of her forever. It took a visit to a psychiatrist, with whom she had developed trust, to crystallize how much our relationship meant to her — how much I meant to her.

Finally, in a change of heart, the meandering, and often exhausting route we had taken to seek financial justice wore me down. I came to the conclusion that continuing my mother's restitution case was far more detrimental than beneficial to her mental health. We discontinued the matter and opted, instead, to pursue the new offer of a quarterly allowance from the Claims Conference to survivors who were in financial hardship. By 1995, my mother was a beneficiary. The quarterly amount provided was about $900 at that time.

My mind could not help but remember the comment of the URO legal representative back in 1965, as though he were asking himself the question — "it is really not clear why a job requiring standing for long periods . . . should promote varicose veins, but standing for roll call in a concentration camp should not." That small reflection represented the confounding nature of the restitution case as well as any other.

In time, my mother emotionally moved on from the case, too tired to continue pursuing a fruitless endeavor and too dedicated to designing her beautiful creations, determined to display her talent until she could no longer push thread through a needle. But I will never discard my anger about the travesty of justice she endured.

The Final Show

A t the end of the first decade of his time in America, when Yussie entered his prepubescent years, his popular shows slowed down to just an occasional event, and then he ceased to perform them altogether. He no longer possessed the visible skeletal outline he'd had as a seven-year-old boy, essential to presenting a proper display of an emaciated specimen. As he grew, his body inevitably began to add fat and muscle, and his filled-out torso could no longer evoke the spirited laughter so anticipated in the past.

The *grine* did not seem to mind that the shows had ceased. No one ever questioned their demise or even requested they be revived with a new featured player. By then, most of them had already moved away from Osgood Street. In addition, Club Hatikvah activities had trickled down to only a few rare occasions. Their days of living near one another, when they could all gather together on short notice, were almost over. They went from being members of a community to being truly independent individuals and families.

As the *grine* acclimated into American culture and became part of the fabric of the American society and economy, they began to come to terms with the horror they had experienced during the Holocaust. While never forgetting what they had endured, they were satisfied with their lives as American citizens. They did not need the reminders of their starved, deprived past to assure them of their safe, comfortable present.

The former bachelors — Mr. Goodman, Mr. Messinger, Mr. Stossel, and Mr. Zwillen — had all married and most of them had children on whom to pin their future hopes. Unfortunately, Mr. Olchinski, rest his soul, never had the opportunity to choose what he felt would be a suitable wife.

Mr. and Mrs. Bach became affluent real estate moguls, buying several apartment buildings and office complexes and renting space to residents and businesses.

The Bialycheks never fully recovered from their illegal incidents. They both moved from job to job over the years until their deaths in the 1980s.

Mrs. Burman, a widow with no children, who often substituted for Mrs. Kester as my caretaker, left Springfield shortly after our move to Forest Park. Her whereabouts, perhaps using her real name or another pseudonym, are unknown.

Mrs. Feinberg, indeed, reconciled with my mother toward the end of her life. She totally forgot the violin incident and renewed the friendship as though it had never occurred. Although she passed away in the 1990s, her husband attained the highest age among the *grine*, succumbing at the age of one hundred and one in 2003.

Mr. and Mrs. Feldman continued their lives together, reconciling to make the best of their earlier ill-fated decision to marry so soon after their liberation. They flourished as business owners and bought their own home in the upscale community of Longmeadow.

Mrs. Fryman, who had come to America with her young son to live near her sister, remarried and bore two more children.

The Kazinskys, who lost their little boy, Benny, in the school bus accident, sadly lost their daughter, Lisa, at the age of five. Their oldest son, Melvin, succumbed to illness when he was only forty years old. I saw Mrs. Kazinsky once more in my adulthood when we met at the funeral of one of the *grine*. She approached me and hugged me tightly but did not speak a word except my name. I never saw her or her husband again.

Mrs. Kester continued to suffer with mental health episodes until her death in the 1970s. Her stories and her double strand of fake pearls are still prominent in my memory.

The Laksers, who had accompanied us on vacation to Moodus, Connecticut, continued their loving relationship until Mr. Lakser's death in the early 1980s and Mrs. Lakser's of a brain aneurysm a few years later.

The Landsmans bought several poultry farms in succession, with some intervening years back in the city, and made a go of it for a while until they were no longer able to compete as small farmers with the large corporate conglomerates and increasing federal regulation. They both passed away in the 1980s.

Mr. Liskowitz was a card player for the rest of his life. His zeal for winning did not diminish at all as he grew older. He finally descended into dementia and passed away in around 2004.

Mrs. Lott remarried about ten years after her husband's death to a short, amiable widower who was born in Lithuania but had come to the United States as a young man after World War I. Mania, her sister-in-law, remarried and moved to Israel with her new husband. Many years later, in the spirit of forever gratitude, the sisters-in-law arranged for Yad Vashem, Israel's living memorial to the Holocaust, to recognize the Polish family that had risked their own lives to save them during the war as "Righteous Among the Nations."

The Posens, the distinguished looking, scholarly couple, continued their daily walks until Mrs. Posen's death in the 1980s. Mr. Posen later remarried a younger Russian immigrant and doted on her until his death of dementia around 2004.

Mr. Rosenlicht, who had kindly warned me of my misguided intentions toward a potential father figure, died recently at the age of ninety-nine in Longmeadow, not too far from our old Springfield neighborhood, having lived more than eight years after his wife's death.

Mrs. Silverstein, the beautiful femme fatale, became a widow in the 1980s. She spent the next few years seeking a new beau or husband. I hope she achieved success.

The Sklarz brothers and their families eventually dispersed to various parts of the country. Two of the brothers and their wives died relatively young, never having seen their grandchildren. Their friends, the Barts and their sons, left for California soon after the big bar mitzvah.

Mr. and Mrs. Stern bought a hardware store in the 1970s and operated it with considerable success until their deaths in the 1990s.

Mr. Stossel and his wife, Rozi, never had children. He died in Brooklyn, New York, in the 1980s. His wife remarried but advised her new husband she could never love anyone else as much as she had loved Mr. Stossel.

Mrs. Zagruder's husband, Mendel, died soon after everyone moved away from Osgood Street. When she remarried a wealthy businessman, she and her two sons relocated to New York, her new husband's home.

My mother, Sidonia Perlstein, began her own design and sewing business in the mid-1960s. Although never attaining great wealth, she became well known in western Massachusetts and northern Connecticut for her remarkable talent, acquiring hundreds of customers for original creations and alterations. Working at her craft until she was almost ninety, she lived longer than most of the *grine*, passing away in 2006 at the age of ninety-three, still keeping most of her secrets to herself. She never married. As she aged, her mental health continued to deteriorate, finally sinking into dementia, when her memories of the Holocaust became more vivid than ever. When shown in her old age a film clip of herself on vacation at Cape Cod with our family, she commented, *Until now, I didn't know den I spik mit an accent.*

What was so funny about the show in the 1950s that all the members of my immigrant community could not wait to see? I believe it was only by laughing in the face of the vision of themselves as victims of depravity that the *grine* could confirm the end of that desolate portion of their lives. They could scoff at their past horrors, set them aside, and put them in their place as something they, indeed, wished to keep in their past, and instead look forward to their own and their children's future. By all accounts, they succeeded far beyond their wildest dreams.

How did their children do in America? They became accountants, bankers, business owners, chief financial officers, doctors, engineers, insurance executives, lawyers, pharmacists, philosophers, psychologists, realtors, scientists, social workers, university professors, and writers. Their profound impact on the world around them, reflective of their parents' high expectations, was inestimable.

As for me, I still wait for further answers to my lifelong quest to know more about the circumstances of my birth. At the same time, I am content with the knowledge I gained through my research into some of my mother's documents and photographs, and from my arduous probe into the repository of my memories. The revelations that came, combined with my revised perceptions of those who constituted my whole world as a young girl, have served to boost my pride in being Sidonia's daughter and a child of the greenhorns. Yet, I have also acquired the secretive, highly private nature of my upbringing — until now.

Acknowledgments

In writing this book and its predecessor, *Sidonia's Thread*, I have relied on a small group of talented, discerning, and loyal friends to provide me with their ideas and suggestions. Their perceptive comments on every aspect of the story were invaluable in shaping the book into its completed form. Each one had her distinctive way of viewing the manuscript and, collectively, helped me to produce the gem that is this book.

My manuscript readers, whom I have always felt possess almost as much ownership in my writing as I do, include Eleanor Beaulieu, Diane DeFronzo, Ellen Frankel, Sue Heller, Beth Stafford, Deborah Stein, Nancy Simonds, Diane Wicks, and Paula Zeiner. Thanks, as always, to all of them for sharing my passion for social justice and for their honest friendship and giving hearts.

I extend my gratitude to Tillie Sheptoff, who remains the best reader in the world, despite the changes that have occurred in her life during the course of my writing. She is still my second mother and most loyal fan.

To Lucile Urvater, two of my grandchildren's *bonne maman*, I offer huge appreciation for taking the time to read my manuscript and applying her teacher's discriminating eye.

My children, Brenda Marcus Bula and Stephen Marcus, who have provided more meaning to my life than words can express, continue to inspire me to write about the extraordinary circumstances of my earlier life. They have both bestowed upon me, with their respective spouses, Michael and Elena, the greatest gifts of all: my grandchildren, Lauren, Sydney, Kate, and Chloe.

I have continued to use the treasure trove of information about my mother's lost family from the United States Holocaust Memorial Museum. "Thank you" to the staff, especially Michlean Amir, of the Holocaust Survivors and Victims Resource Center, for their meticulous work. The information contained in these formerly unavailable records from the International Tracing Service has changed my life forever.

Many thanks to my childhood rabbi, David Edelman, who passed away during the course of my writing this book, only one day after his ninetieth birthday, for showing me the way of righteousness and for his original support for the words in *Sidonia's Thread*, some of which reappear in these pages.

My experience with Yiddish translator Mark Newton was both enjoyable and edifying. Armed as I was with a little knowledge of Yiddish, I tested his patience in sparring about the meanings and connotations of particular words and phrases contained in certain documents. Not only were the letters written in transliterated Yiddish in the Latin alphabet rather than the more commonly used Hebrew alphabet, they were written in a Hungarian speaker's "voice," with its idiosyncratic grammar and spelling. Mark ultimately produced a highly satisfactory and insightful translation of the four Yiddish letters contained in this book.

Thanks to Beth Richards, who applied her proofreading skill to each and every word and phrase for overlooked errors in grammar, punctuation, language, and the tiny things in an author's copy that require an expert eye.

Stefano Bucciarelli performed a skillful job in translating one of the most important letters written in German contained in the last chapter of this book, which pertains to my mother's restitution case. His willingness to study and research the full meaning of the legal finding in the letter changed my view of the factors that led to my mother's frustrating journey to find justice. I thank him for his expertise and perseverance.

Carol Powers, my developmental editor, consistently challenged me to focus on the content of my manuscript and suggested structural changes to strengthen the story and focus on my target audience. Her professional judgment had a profound effect on the final product of this book.

Finally, I owe an immense debt of gratitude to my editor, Lorraine Alexson. After her masterful editing of *Sidonia's Thread*, I was convinced that her touches to the story were one of the prime factors in its extraordinary success. She has been a constant source of strength and benevolent yet sage advice about the writing process and the decision-making that goes into creating a finely tuned literary piece. Possessing the skill of a craftsperson and the sensibility of an artist, she is certainly among the best of her profession.